"A dynamic and hope-filled book to provoke the ecclesial imagination. May it help us grow closer to God's dream for the church."

Shane Claiborne, activist, author,
The Irresistible Revolution: Living as an Ordinary Radical

"*Signs of Emergence* is one of the most insightful books available on the subject of the emergent church. With a concise yet pastoral message, Brewin guides the reader through a dynamic understanding of this major movement. This book has the potential to blow the emerging church conversation wide open."

Will Samson, coauthor, *Justice in the Burbs:*
Being the Hands of Jesus Wherever You Live

"*Signs of Emergence* is a rich and luminous meditation on the nature of change, which is grounded in a deep understanding of the Christian narrative and a keen insight into the structure of organic development. With his eyes fixed firmly upon both the wonder of Christ and the wonder of nature, Kester Brewin offers us a way of rethinking and reorganizing church structures in a radical way that dances between the dangers of rigidity on the one hand and anarchy on the other. In this book we are encouraged to form fluid, 'dirty,' and generous structures that celebrate the virtues of openness, change, and adaptation."

—Peter Rollins, author, *How (Not) to Speak of God*;
founder, Ikon community

"*Signs of Emergence* is one of those rare books that manages to combine deep theological reflection, new science perspectives, and creative ecclesiology with a genuine element of originality. Kester Brewin has fertilized the Western church's dulled imagination with this fine work."

—Alan Hirsch, author, *The Forgotten Ways:*
Reactivating the Missional Church; founding director,
Forge Mission Training Network

"Kester Brewin invites us on a risky journey to leave behind a church that finds itself marginalized in a society that views it as increasingly irrelevant. Brewin invites us to join those on the emerging edge in rediscovering the church as a 'constantly reforming, learning community.' This is an invitation to wait, listen, and witness the new to which God is giving birth . . . from the bottom up. I predict this book will stimulate a very important conversation regarding the future of the church in the West. *Signs of Emergence* will prove an invaluable academic resource for those in leadership who are seeking to re-imagine new expressions of the church in a changing world."

—Tom Sine, Mustard Seed Associates

"In these pages are perceptive and loving words about the church, rooted in an understanding of its reality but without the need to develop idealized, romantic notions of what the church was at some point in time, then read back onto the present. Here is someone who offers important frameworks from development and emergence theory to offer churches a way of understanding how all of us can navigate the tough waters of change. I appreciate the way this book honors existing churches without shying away from the challenges they face. Brewin doesn't write 'almost hopeless' over these churches; he encourages by offering guidance through a difficult transition."

—Alan Roxburgh, coauthor, *The Missional Leader: Equipping Your Church to Reach a Changing World*; president, Missional Leadership Institute

"Beautifully weaving theory and praxis, Kester Brewin has a gift for the church: by looking closely at the rhythms of the crucified life and intersections with rhythms of the city, he gives us a new way forward as Christ-followers. This is a thoughtful and thought-provoking book."

—Tony Jones, national coordinator, Emergent Village; author, *The Sacred Way: Spiritual Practices for Everyday Life*

"My friend Kester Brewin writes with a wise, gentle, and prophetic voice, offering a perspective on the future of the church in the Western world that is at once incisive and hopeful."

—Mark Scandrette, author, *Soul Graffiti: Making a Life in the Way of Jesus*; senior fellow, Emergent Village

"Through Kester Brewin's eyes, pilgrims can see cities as the place where one's dreamy theologies and 'psycho-spiritual bull' confronts the Concrete Christ. A highly recommended faith journey for those who dare to walk the walk and follow the trouble-making Jesus."

—Becky Garrison, senior contributing editor and author,
Rising from the Ashes: Rethinking Church (forthcoming)

"One of the best books written on the emerging church."

—Jordon Cooper, founding member, Resonate; church planter,
Saskatoon, Saskatchewan, Canada

"A fabulous book—original, creative, stimulating, provocative."

—Jonny Baker, coauthor, *Alternative Worship:
Resources from and for the Emerging Church*

"Kester Brewin writes the way he lives—at the intersection between intelligent theology and integrated living. *Signs of Emergence* is a revolutionary statement of intent: Jesus lives where the dirt is, which is good news for all of us, even if our religious institutions haven't realized the implications yet. Reading this book will challenge your own boundaries. If you let it do its work, you will never be the same again."

—Gareth Higgins, activist, author, *How Movies Helped
Save My Soul: Finding Spiritual Fingerprints in
Culturally Significant Films*

"Kester Brewin is one of the sharpest thinkers on the emerging scene. For years, his community, Vaux, created worship spaces that engaged forbidden cultural and theological themes. His book *Signs of Emergence* continues this pattern and doesn't disappoint. Brewin combines psychology, urban theory, and complexity theory with biblical reflection on church and leadership. The result? A fresh look at the contemporary scene with an innovative approach to leadership in the church. Expect your imagination to be stimulated to think new thoughts about the church in the world today."

—Ryan Bolger, assistant professor of church in
contemporary culture, Fuller Theological Seminary;
coauthor, *Emerging Churches: Creating Christian
Community in Postmodern Cultures*

émersion

An Emergent Manifesto of Hope
edited by Doug Pagitt and Tony Jones

Organic Community
Joseph R. Myers

Signs of Emergence
Kester Brewin

Justice in the Burbs
Will and Lisa Samson (August 2007)

Intuitive Leadership
Tim Keel (Fall 2007)

Losing My Religion
Samir Selmanovic

www.emersionbooks.com

signs of
Emergence

A Vision for Church That Is Organic/**Networked**
Decentralized/Bottom-Up/**Communal**/Flexible
{ Always Evolving }

Kester Brewin

BakerBooks
Grand Rapids, Michigan

© 2004, 2007 by Kester Brewin

Published by Baker Books
a division of Baker Publishing Group
P.O. Box 6287, Grand Rapids, MI 49516-6287
www.bakerbooks.com

Previously published in the UK in 2004 under the title *The Complex Christ: Signs of Emergence in the Urban Church* by SPCK

Printed in the United States of America

Library of Congress Cataloging-in-Publication Data
Brewin, Kester, 1972–
    [Complex Christ]
    Signs of emergence : a vision for church that is organic/networked/decentralized/bottom-up/communal/flexible/always evolving / Kester Brewin.
        p.   cm.
    Originally published : Complex Christ, England, 2004.
    Includes bibliographical references.
    ISBN 10: 0-8010-6808-8 (pbk.)
    ISBN 978-0-8010-6808-9 (pbk.)
    1. Church renewal. 2. Church growth. 3. Change (Psychology)—Religious aspects—Christianity. 4. Postmodernism—Religious aspects—Christianity. 5. Mission of the church. I. Title.
    BV600.3.B74 2007
    262.0017—dc22   2007005638

In keeping with biblical principles of creation stewardship, Baker Publishing Group advocates the responsible use of our natural resources. As a member of the Green Press Initiative, our company uses recycled paper when possible. The text paper of this book is comprised of 30% post-consumer waste.

117612

{ Contents }

Preface to the US Edition 11
Preface to the UK Edition 15
Acknowledgments 17
Introduction 19

Part 1: Advent / Incarnation / Emergence
1 Advent 41
2 Incarnation 59
3 Emergence 73

Interlude: The Character of the Emergent Church
4 The Character of the Emergent Church 91

Part 2: Cities / Gift / Dirt
5 Cities 121
6 Gift 145
7 Dirt 165

Conclusion: The Emergence of Christ
8. The Emergence of Christ 187

Postscript 203
Notes 205
Further Reading 215

{ Preface to the US Edition }

Just over two years ago, I sat down to pen the foreword to *The Complex Christ*—the UK edition of the book you are now holding. There I reflected on the parallels between two "births": releasing my first book and welcoming into the world my first child. Now, with a second child on the way as I write this new foreword, I am drawn again to think on the things we bring to birth: the lives they begin to lead, the movement to independence, the struggles to communicate, and the inheritances they carry.

So as I write, it's with a hope that the words that follow—which were written in 2004 in the context of my own UK situation—will travel well across the Atlantic, find a life there and find places to resonate.

Personally, I'm very excited about the prospect of this book reaching a wider US audience, mainly because so many of the ideas and books that inspired me came from the US in the first place. It is one of the paradoxes of our time that the USA has taken so much bad press for fundamentalist religion mixed with power politics and authoritarian structures, and yet has led the world in the development of the new science of emergence and the ideas behind self-organization and distributed leadership.

So there is a sense in which this book, which explores the thesis that in the incarnation we see God "re-emerging," is "coming home" to the land where some wonderful, interconnected free thinking has explored how deeply rooted in emergent systems our cities and ecosystems are.

Many of you will be aware of the use of the word *emergent* in different contexts, and one of those contexts may well be the network of individuals and groups who have taken that umbrella name as they explore new forms of being church. Ironically, and perhaps providentially, at the time I wrote the book I was unaware such a network even existed. The term *emerging church* had, even by then, begun to lose any useful meaning in the UK, and so, wanting to relocate some of the language in a more meaningful place, I chose the term *emergent church* to describe the bottom-up, self-organizing communities that I proposed might be a way forward.

My use of the term *emergent* does not therefore presuppose any link with any Emergent structures or people, but I hope you will be able to pick up a sense of shared spirit between the two meanings. Moreover, I hope that the sense in which I have used the term will retain some of its porous nature, and will offer some fresh perspectives on the movement as it approaches a decade or so of existence. As with all such movements, there are natural stages—the excitement of conception and birth, the freedom of infancy, and the difficulties of coming of age. Who are we? What are we doing? Was this really what we set out to create?

Such questions are entirely natural, and highly appropriate. As this emerging church movement ages, there are bound to be those within it who will feel it has "denominated" too far from them, and who want to push the boundaries further, while others want to spend time properly maturing in the new ground that has been explored. In short, taking a theme from the chapter on "Dirt," there will be those who want to play trickster with the emerging conversation, even as it has recently played trickster with the established church. We should not fear this trickster work, for we should have learned that its apparent contamination of our faith may actually hold its renewal and re-formation within it.

It is this idea of a constantly re-forming, learning community that is one of the driving passions behind this book. We have for too long been trapped in cycles of boom or bust: hailing each new movement as the be-all and end-all of faith, only to slam it into the ground in a flurry of burnt-out ministers and angry members a few years later.

It need not be this way.

As we seek genuine newness, as we seek the renewal of our faith and a fresh way forward in an increasingly post-Christian West, we must restrain ourselves from being too quickly critical of the successes or failures of emerging congregations. Instead, we must attempt to form them as learning communities, with the mechanisms for their regular renewal built into them, and seek to commit ourselves to the relationships within them, rather than the structures around them.

This is one of the beauties of a faith built on death and resurrection. The body of Christ will continue, eternally. But these little bodies that we build, trying to bring some structure and rhythm to the relationships we share, need not carry on forever. While the relationships continue underneath, the vehicles we commandeer to take us on various stages of our journey will zoom and splutter and will—sometimes—need abandoning. This has certainly been my experience in the communities I have journeyed with, and I suspect that we will see many more emerging churches, or umbrella groups, fail in the coming years. In a healthy learning environment, such things ought not to be perceived as failure (though many may want to spin it that way); rather the shedding of an old skin, to allow the inhabitation of a new one, better fit for purpose.

So, in this book, when you read about stopping, finishing, ending, I hope you are able to see that this is an exercise in hope, rather than despair. It is desperate if we can imagine nothing will ever change; we are, on the other hand, filled with hope if we believe that Christ is still desperate to incarnate himself in every myriad community in every changing season.

Chesterton's famous quote comes to mind: "It is not that Christianity has been tried and found wanting, rather it is that it has been found too difficult left untried." It is my prayer that as we come to what may be a difficult age in this "emerging conversation," we may not give up trying, but make those decisions we know are difficult; it is my deepest fear that we may look back in the future with sadness and realize we didn't grasp this opportunity. Having met some of the brave and godly women and men in the church in the US over the past few years, I am hopeful that my fears will be unfounded.

Finally, the irony of releasing a book—a solid object, with words inked indelibly—with the phrase "always evolving" in the title is not lost on me. Committing fluid thoughts to text renders them immediately more bounded and less free, and, if I were rewriting the whole book now, there are probably thoughts I would solidify in a different way. We can worry about these things too much; given that our thinking is always evolving, a "finished" book is an unattainable ideal. We have to stop somewhere and let the type set. So these printed thoughts on an always evolving model of church shouldn't be taken as final. Indeed, I'd encourage you to come and join the more democratic and immediate discussion on http://kester.typepad.com/signs.

Kester Brewin
2006

{ Preface to the UK Edition }

It has been said that "journeys are the midwives of our thoughts," and for always encouraging me to think in new ways, this book is dedicated to Dad, who once waved me off on a journey with the words "Don't do anything I wouldn't do," and thus gave me an awful lot of scope.

I am keenly aware of the possibilities of language, and the myriad different ways that these ideas could have been put across. With this in mind, I offer this opening prayer in the hope that what I have written will speak some truth:

> The fish-trap exists because of the fish.
> Once you've got the fish, the trap can be forgotten.
> Words exist because of meaning.
> Once you've got the meaning, the words can be
> forgotten.
>
> Chuang Tzu

{ Acknowledgments }

Norman Mailer once quipped that "writing a book is the closest a man will ever get to having a baby," so I must first thank Beki a thousand times for her loving support in enduring this literary pregnancy, while coping so amazingly with her own very real ones. I couldn't have done it without you; this one's for Iris Frankie.

Thanks also to everyone around Vaux—the ship that has carried me to so many interesting shores—and Greenbelt Festival for supporting the idea financially.

In the summer of 2006 I was privileged enough to spend some time sharing at the "Soliton Sessions" in Ventura, CA. For all their amazing hospitality and inspiration, I want to dedicate this US edition to everyone at Soliton, and Greg and Michelle in particular.

{ Introduction }

This is a book about change. More specifically, it is an attempt to resource the church with some ideas about how change happens, and how these ideas might be applied to our faith. If Christianity is to remain "vital," then it is, in the truest sense, "vital" that we understand change: for an organism to show signs of life, it must show it can respond to its environment, and for the church to retain a vibrancy about its faith, it must "adapt and survive."

Even if there is little evidence of change visible to the external observer, the process of the church thinking is a healthy sign that we know that things cannot stay as they are. Descartes boiled the bare facts of his existence down to *"Je pense, donc je suis"*;[1] he could equally have written that the thoughtless are dead. That the church is coming to grips with thinking is in itself encouraging, even if the physical manifestations of change are few and far between.

From biology to economics, science concurs: to stop changing is to die. Mike Riddell has written starkly of his belief that "the Christian church is dying in the West."[2]

It would be foolish to disagree with his diagnosis, but I am proposing that a more healthy prognosis is available: this death of the church, and the accompanying death of the historic Christian culture, can be avoided if we are prepared to do some serious thinking and soul-searching. It has perhaps been our reluctance to think, and thus our slowness to change and respond to a civilization that since the Industrial Revolution has phenomenally accelerated (increased its rate of change), that has put us in this near-death situation.

The question, then, is not shall we change, but how to do so. And if change is equivalent to life, then the way one leads one's life needs to be informed by the nature of change. "How can we effect transformation?" is thus a question of the most profound importance. Little wonder that it is a problem that has troubled the minds of philosophers, economists, sociologists, and politicians for centuries.

Unfortunately, the church's answer seems to have focused, perhaps not surprisingly in our culture so obsessed with the self, on personal change as the route to its revitalization. We have been told by our leaders that "revival" will come just as soon as our individual personal holiness ratings reach a certain saintly mark. The resuscitation of the dying church has been made out to be dependent on the sinlessness of its members, yet we have to ask the question: did the leavers all go in the first place because we weren't holy enough? Of course not. They left because it was boring, unchanging, irrelevant, said nothing to them about their life, and was completely unconnected to their experience. A recent Church of England report into fresh expressions of church concluded that the unchurched don't come to church because they see church as "peripheral, obscure, confusing or irrelevant."[3] From my conversations with church leaders in the US, I

20

sense that the same conclusion could be reached about the American unchurched.

To blame the demise of the church on personal holiness is a dangerous and wrong position. I believe that rather than focusing on changing our individual lives, we need to change our corporate practice. New wine is currently being wasted by ruptured wineskins, and it is outrageous to ask the workers to keep pressing grapes when the vineyard keeps pouring it into old skins, allowing them to rupture and spill the newness into the drains.

To use an example from politics, we have become a party unelectable. The faithful on the ground try desperately to talk policy and engage in debate with voters, while the party leaders fall out, backbite, and point fingers. One can always tell that an institution is in trouble when infighting starts and those at the top begin to lose sight of the outside world, focusing all their energies on internal wrangling, seemingly determined to pull the house down around them rather than lose face. It is not the party faithful in the constituencies who are losing us elections, but the very structure of the party institutions, and it is here that we must set the locus of change.

Another example springs to mind from my degree studies in Bristol. From a course designed to enhance problem-solving and creative-thinking skills, one of the few things that has stuck with me over the years is a mantra that our lecturer used to pepper us with every week: "If the people who built the railroads in the United States were actually interested in transporting people, they would now own the airlines." But they don't. The industrial historians tell us that the reason for this is that once the railroad companies had completed the huge task of driving the lines across the US, they lost their focus. Instead of continuing to pioneer ways of allowing free movement of people, they lost sight of the key *end* and focused internally on the one *means* to that end that they had made.

For a century or so, this was no problem because the railroad was still the best way to get around, but with the advent of the airlines the railroad companies were overtaken by a mode of transport that was massively better. And, as our lecturer warned us in grave tones, their customers flocked to it.

Or, at least, most of them did. Perhaps the reason this story stuck in my mind was that the more times he repeated it, the more I reflected that there were still a few old romantics who just loved the railroad and who continued to dress up in their finery, climb aboard, and drift along gently, buttressing each other with talk of how the railroad was the *proper* way to travel, not like this fancy airline stuff. They assured each other everything was going to be just fine, while the planes full of people shot by overhead.

What the railroad owners failed to appreciate is that if you are to "keep the main thing the main thing," as the management-speak goes, it is highly likely that at some point you are going to have to fundamentally change the way you operate, and this will probably involve having to deconstruct the very modus operandi that you are currently using. I am sure there are those who claim a revival in the railroads would come about as soon as the station staff and conductors were more polite and behaved better. They miss the point. The reason people don't use the railroad is not because of the attitude of those who run it but because its method of transporting people from one place to another has been superseded.

People love to talk of revival, but fail to grasp that things that need reviving are by definition close to death. Yes, I believe the church needs to pray for revival, but I would like to reclaim the word from the ribbon-dancers and charismatic sensationalists. When we talk of revival we should not

22

think of some joyous time with thronging masses of people spontaneously coming to our doors. Rather, we should wince at the prospect of the rib-cracking pain of emergency resuscitation as this dying body is shaken back to life. Put the discipleship books back on the shelves for a while and get down to the drawing board, for this is not going to happen through an upsurge in personal holiness but by a radical transformation of our corporate practice.

The Chapel

A little aside from the main road,
Becalmed in a last-century greyness,
there is the chapel, ugly, without the appeal
to the tourist to stop his car
and visit it. The traffic goes by,
and the river goes by, and quick shadows
of clouds, too, and the chapel settles
a little deeper into the grass.

But here once on an evening like this,
in the darkness that was about
his hearers, a preacher caught fire
and burned steadily before them
with a strange light, so that they saw
the splendour of the barren mountains
about them and sang their amens
fiercely, narrow but saved
in a way that men are not now.

R. S. Thomas[4]

Change is life, and transformation is vital. We know that personal change alone will not do, and that root and branch corporate reform is needed, but the question remains: how can transformation be achieved? To return to politics for a moment, there seem to be two schools of thought: change is effected by either *legislation* or *education*. Imagine, for example, that a government wanted to stop people driving their gas-guzzling four-by-fours within city limits. It could either pass a law to criminalize those who did or try to educate people as to why doing so was damaging to the environment generally, and the life of the city in particular. Both means would, ideally, achieve the same end, but one way would be "top-down" and leave people no choice, while the other would be "bottom-up" and preserve people's essential freedom. Legislation is about the exercise of power; education is about the exercise of empowerment.

I believe that for too long we have allowed those in love with authority to attempt to legislate for change: to attempt transformation by the exercise of power. It is clear in the power struggles going on in the worldwide church that this has served to do great damage, leaving people criminalized, feeling unloved, guilty, and excluded. There needs to be another way, for this is clearly not the way of Christ. I want to argue that the transformation of the church will be about empowering people to face the fundamental questions of their local existence, engaging with all its complexity and emerging as a renewed organism that is faithful to the truth but disinterested in power.

The problem with the legislative answer to transformation is that it throws a wide, general net that ends up catching far more than it was designed to. The advantage of the "bottom-up" approach to change is that it evolves out of debate from people on the ground, whose behavior is transformed from within. This allows them to assimilate the full complexities of their local situation into their solutions.

It is this complexity with which we are concerned. It is not presented in contrast to simplicity; rather, it is about the rich and beautifully complex depths of things that can evolve when the simple fundamentals are held together and not ignored. As Oliver Wendell Holmes once said, "For the simplicity on this side of complexity, I wouldn't give you a fig. But for the simplicity on the other side of complexity, for that I would give you anything I have."[5] Answers that do not acknowledge the full reality and complexity of our situation are essentially futile. We need to be in love with the ancient wisdom of simplicity, yet not allow ourselves to become simplistic; to be prepared to journey with an "emergent Christ"—a Christ who entered our world and evolved a new faith from the ground up.

An excellent example of this bottom-up approach to change, where simple fundamentals lead to complex solutions, can be found in the slightly daunting world of computer programming, and in a man called Danny Hillis, who constructed a program that completely undermined the very foundations of writing software. It is a story that I believe is pertinent to our situation.

One of the benchmark tests for any programming language is number-sorting. Throw 100 random numbers at a computer, and see how many steps it takes to sort them into numerical order. Anyone can do it in 99 steps, but for programmers it is all about maximizing the efficiency of processors, and this number-sorting conundrum is a simple logic problem that can be used to test out all their programming ingenuity. By the time Hillis came to the problem, the record was 66 steps. However, rather than sit down and try to write a new piece of software from the top down, he instead took a very powerful computer and instructed it to generate thousands of miniprograms, which were made up of simple instructions selected completely randomly. Each of these miniprograms was then tested to see if it showed any ability at all at number-sorting. If it did, it survived to the next generation and was bred with another miniprogram—their codes were combined and slightly mutated to create a new miniprogram. In the couple of minutes it took the computer to perform a few thousand cycles of this process, the code had evolved into a program that could sort numbers in 75 steps.

This was impressive, but Hillis was disappointed; no matter how many times he repeated the experiment, he could never get the computer to generate a program that did much better than 75 steps.

Hillis's genius was to realize that his system was facing the same hurdle that many evolutionary systems do: it had reached a local maximum. Imagine all the infinite possibilities of number-sorting programs mapped out as a physical landscape. Like the Himalayas, there will be deep valleys—which represent the least successful programs—and tall peaks—which represent the more successful ones. What Hillis's software was doing was blindly exploring that landscape, looking for steep sides going up toward peaks. Yet, being "blind," once a miniprogram had reached a peak, any peak, it stopped evolving and thought it was on top of the world. It had no way of appreciating that there were thousands of low peaks in these virtual Himalayas, but only one Everest.

To get over this evolutionary problem, Hillis introduced a natural solution: predators. With his revised system, once a miniprogram had reached a local maximum of, say, 75 steps, it became at risk of being destroyed by a predator program if it stayed there, so it was forced off its peak, chased down to lower ground and then required to find a higher peak by mutating its code again. Running this system, Hillis came out with a program that could sort numbers in 62 steps, an improvement on the previous best of 66 steps that, in the computer world, was akin to knocking whole seconds off the 100-meter sprint record. Yet he had not done so by writing the code himself. All he had done was set up the simple initial conditions and allowed the complexities of the program to emerge from the bottom up.

It is my belief that most manifestations of church have reached a "local maximum." The evolutionary processes that molded them and nudged them certain ways toward their styles of worship and modes of being actually originated in small country churches of hundreds of years ago. They developed to meet the needs of the Industrial Revolution and have continued to seek out higher ground, but in the new situation of the post-Christian West, we are beginning to see that this animal is now unfit for its environment. Within the confines of the model that we have been using, there is no more room for improvement; the church cannot advance further along this branch. While individuals have been told that the answer to the question "How can we effect transformation?" lies in personal holiness, the systemic faults that are actually the root of the problem have remained unchanged.

God's track record suggests little time for ecclesiastic culs-de-sac or local spiritual highs. To stand still and stop evolving is eventually to be left behind and face extinction. More poignantly, not to appreciate that you *are* evolving and not to be prepared to admit changes that have occurred have the same end result.

Although some of us may be more conscious of it than others, we all change and experience different phases in our beliefs, both as individuals and communities, as James Fowler has described in his book *Stages of Faith: The Psychology of Human Development and the Quest for Meaning*. Of the six he identifies, the first two stages (Intuitive-Projective and Mythical-Literal) describe the rather childlike understanding that we may have of God. At Stage 1 a child might have a view based on fantasy or what they have picked up from TV; by Stage 2 they are beginning to take on the stories and beliefs of the community and are able to solidify them into some sort of narrative. It is at Stage 3 (Synthetic-Conventional) that many Christians and churches seem to have found a local maximum. Indeed Fowler comments that

27

"for many adults it becomes a permanent place of equilibrium" where people fall into the trap of thinking that any further change is unnecessary.[6] At this stage being part of a *tribe* or community is very significant. Reflecting on Fowler's work, Alan Jamieson identifies people at this stage as being "loyalists who hold deep convictions" but that

> while their beliefs and values are often deeply held they are typically not examined critically and are therefore tacitly held to. That is, they know what they know but are generally unable to tell you how they know something is true except by referring to an external authority outside of themselves. The most common examples of this are "the Bible says so," or "my pastor teaches this."[7]

Many Christians have moved beyond this "loyalist" phase to Stage 4, to what Fowler calls the Individuative-Reflective stage, where they begin to critique the beliefs, teachings, and practices of the group. It is a loss of innocence, a realization that the truth is more complex than we thought. In his classic work *Orthodoxy*, G. K. Chesterton describes the beginnings of such a realization:

> Suppose some mathematical creature from the moon were able to reckon up the human body: he would at once see that it was duplicate. Having noted that there was an arm on the right and one on the left, a leg on the right and one on the left, he might go further and still find on each side the same number of fingers, the same number of toes, twin eyes, twin ears, twin nostrils, and even twin lobes on the brain. At last he would take it as a law; and then, where he found a heart on one side, would deduce that there was another heart on the other. And just then, where he felt he was right, he would be wrong. . . . Life is not an illogicality, yet it is a trap for logicians; its inexactitude lies hidden; its wildness lies in wait.[8]

Stage 4 is about the realization that what lies beneath the apparent simplicity of faith is unsymmetrical complexity.

Anyone who has been through this stage, or knows someone who has, will know that it can be lonely and protracted. People at Stage 4 can make life very difficult for any groups they are a part of. They raise doubts and call things into question. Their identity does not need to be bolstered by being part of a tribe, and they tend to widen their frame of reference beyond the perceived small world of Stage 3. For these reasons, churches that are stuck around Stage 3 become intolerant of those in Stage 4, who in turn become intolerant of an unchanging church, and many, many Christians give up and leave the church altogether.

Stage 4 is akin to the necessary movement down from the local maximum back into the valleys. What Hillis was effectively requiring of his miniprograms was to move beyond their narrow confidence of Stage 3 and experience what St. John of the Cross described as the "Dark Night of the Soul." It is a hard and narrow path that mystics from every creed agree is an essential part of the road to mature faith. We see it in the narrative of virtually every film: the innocent opening, the crisis that must be faced in the middle, before the ending where our protagonists are more knowing and wise. It is only once we have been through this difficulty, this darkness of Stage 4, that we have any chance of gaining higher ground—what Fowler would call the Conjunctive Stage 5.

Stage 5 is a place of humility, with none of the brash arrogance of Stage 3; a place where the doubts and criticisms of Stage 4 are not extinguished, but the self is able to hold things in tension and appreciate mystery. Fowler describes the emergence of Stage 5 as akin to the realization that the behavior of light requires it to be understood simultaneously as a wave *and* a particle, even though this is rationally impossible. He describes people at this stage as having a deep simplicity, yet realizing the "organic and interconnected character of things." If Stage 3 is one-dimensional, and Stage 4 a place where the very idea of dimensions is questioned, then Stage 5 is a place where "in its richness, ambiguity, and multidimensionality, truth must be approached from at least two or more angles of vision simultaneously," and where "faith . . . gives rise to a second naïveté [and] readiness for participation."[9] If this is not the actual Everest that so few manage to reach, it is at least the beginnings of the climb back up, but with the wisdom that more valleys may yet be faced.

Beyond Stage 5, which Fowler doubts many reach before middle age, comes the "universalizing" of Stage 6. This stage is how we might describe the Gandhis, Mother Teresas, Martin Luther Kings, and Thomas Mertons. These people are not perfect, but

> in their penetration through the obsession with survival, security and significance they threaten our measured standards of righteousness and goodness and prudence. . . . Universalisers are often experienced as subversive of the structures by which we maintain our individual and corporate survival, security and significance. Many persons at this stage die at the hands of those whom they hope to change.[10]

There are few who make it here.

One of my concerns, both in my work in education and in dealings with the church, is that we are in danger of failing to progress through these stages; that we are stalling after the more childlike stages and are being caught in a cultural and spiritual infantilism. That our society worships youth and youthful beauty, and is suffering unprecedented levels of pedophilia, are two sides of the same problem. We see in the church too many people trying, through events for youth, to live inside a world they clearly do not belong in, while not allowing those who do live there opportunities to lead. We seem afraid of growing up, wary of maturity, and the responsibilities and complexities that it will bring, and so attempt to hide ourselves inside wrinkle-free skins and simplistic solutions. Because the essential connections that should allow the transfer of knowledge between the generations have been wrecked by an arrogant culture of adolescence, we deny the sagacious old of our communities the chance to pass on their wisdom, and so make the same mistakes they did. The means by which people can be led to more mature stages are being left like paths untrod and overgrown, condemning us to a constant diet of milk, unable to progress to the solid foods of the latter stages. It is vital that the paths between these stages remain mapped, and that communication between those at different points along them is kept open. There is no point climbing to the peaks if you deny anyone else the opportunity to follow you up, and it is only by doing this that we have any hope of truly becoming wise, without having to relearn everything for ourselves.

From a wider sociological standpoint, in his more recent book *Faithful Change: The Personal and Public Challenges of Postmodern Life*, Fowler has paralleled the ascent up the more adult stages of faith with the movement of Western society from a pre-Enlightenment to a post-Enlightenment era. Flying in the face of those who have commonly located the Western church in the "modern" era of the Enlightenment, Fowler suggests that "the Synthetic-Conventional [Stage 3] form of faith consciousness can be seen as having rootage in and preserving important elements of pre-Enlightenment forms of cultural consciousness."[11] Thus the faith consciousness of such Stage 3 churches would be defined as tacit, with an external locus of authority usually "in sacred texts or in the group's authorized representatives."[12] Organizationally, these churches have hierarchical authority and information control "with leadership elites enjoying the same implicit sanction of natural or divinely ordained authorization."[13]

The modern, or Enlightenment, era that many have claimed to be the natural ground for much of the Western church, evangelical or otherwise, thus in Fowler's analysis is actually paralleled to the Individuative-Reflective Stage 4 outlined above. It is here that external loci of authority are called into question, and life is criticized from a scientific perspective. The Enlightenment was a period of demythologizing, where the powers of objectivity were emphasized, and a kind of sovereign privilege was given to the critical and reflective deliberations of the individual; thus we see at this stage believers calling into question and doubting many of the tacitly held beliefs of the Stage 3 church.

Hence the post-Enlightenment era that we have begun to explore as a society since some time after the Second World War is paralleled by Fowler to the Conjunctive Stage 5. Its description as "conjunctive" comes from Carl Jung's appropriation of the term to mean the ability to hold opposites together in a single frame, and we see this as a strong theme in post-Enlightenment culture. It is a movement beyond the simplistic, externally authorized local peak of Stage 3 belief, through and beyond the critical, lonely valley of Stage 4's individuative "dark night," and out into the second naïveté of Stage 5 where the complexities of life are held together, and where hierarchies have given way to networks of organization. Fowler's plea in *Faithful Change* is for us to

> work consciously and effectively at nurturing and supporting a substantial minority, a *political and cultural leadership group*, who embrace their faith in terms of the structures of the *practical postmodern* stance of faith in this time of

transition in cultural consciousness. The first task . . . is that of nurturing and supporting political and cultural leaders prepared to *claim and model Conjunctive faith*.[14]

It is important to note that one can never force individuals from stage to stage. It is no good egging someone on to Stage 4; what is important is that the path is clear for them to travel when they find their way there in their own time. In fact, it would be criminal to force people on before they were ready, for Fowler suggests that it is usually difficulties or suffering that prompt movement, and to wish that someone would just suffer a bit so that they could see the truth better is unthinkable. The problems come when people are either so enmeshed in their infantilism and disconnected from wiser sources that they never find out that other paths exist, or are spiritually unconscious and unable to process the changes they are experiencing. If people are forced to experience life from a Stage 3 perspective in a Stage 3 church when they are actually at Stage 4 (but have no idea that anything could be different), then they are likely to become damaged. Two things tend to happen at this point: either they opt out altogether or, like infants and the railroad owners, blindly focus all their energies on making the only model they know work as best it can, not realizing that any other is possible.

The concern of this book is to try to show that not only is another model possible but essential. While it is not right to force people from stage to stage, I do believe it is vital that we strongly encourage our institutions to move on from the Stage 3 in which many of them are caught.[15] Like Fowler, I believe that if we are to impact the post-Enlightenment cultural consciousness, then we must be modeling a conjunctive faith in a conjunctive church, for it is only in such a place that people from *all* stages can experience community and growth together.

33

An example from art may be illuminating. Imagine a group of people looking at a picture. Some will be looking straight on, from a single perspective and angle, and declaring that this is surely the most obvious and rational way of seeing. But others will become bored by this view, and want to investigate the structure of the work more closely in the minutiae of brush techniques and minor canvas defects. They will claim that a simplistic viewing is mindless without taking these real problems into account. Neither group will be of much help to each other, and they will likely end up arguing.

What the conjunctive view will be able to do—which fits Jung's usage perfectly—is to bring a more mature way of seeing to both groups. Drawing on the historical perspective and knowledge of other works, the conjunctive observer will hopefully be able to move everyone to a deeper love and appreciation of the work in a way that they could not do alone or even together.

Beyond the goal of showing that systemic change is vital, that a new, conjunctive way of seeing is needed, this book is also a heartfelt petition to the church to see that the means must fit the ends: the *route* to change must not be through the exercise of power but through an exercise in empowerment. This book is not just a plea for the church stuck at Stage 3 to move on and return to the valleys below; it is a plea that the model of leadership of the church on this difficult path must not be the same model that led it there in the first place. If I am right in saying that many churches have reached a "local maximum," then it is vital to their health and survival as communities that they not only appreciate where they are at and know that change is possible, but also are empowered to do something about it in a new way. For this reason, I am going to use the term the *Emergent Church* for what Fowler calls the "Conjunctive Church." It is easy to agree that we want to become conjunctive, but I believe that the science of emergence (discussed in depth in chapter 3) offers us real hope in discovering how we might do it.

The distinction between this Emergent Church and the much discussed *emerging church* is an important one, which is discussed in chapter 4; suffice it to say for now that it is more than semantics. The *emerging church* is a label that is being stuck on anything outside the "norms" of the church as most people know it; whereas the *Emergent Church* is specifically about the principles of the science of emergence to church growth.

The principle of emergence is all about bottom-up change.

If we have been guilty of not progressing through the stages mentioned above, it may be because the energy levels that leaders have been able to summon and focus, from the top down, simply have been not high enough. It is my belief that the required energy will only be summoned when we work together, from the bottom up, rather than leaving it all up to the solitary professionals, who end up burning out. But the journey toward this new way of channeling our energy is a daunting one, one that will require us to completely change the mode of organization that we have been using. Doubtless many will try to live in denial and claim that this energy state, this molecular arrangement, this local peak, is the place God wants us to stay, but the wisdom of history, of seers such as St. John of the Cross, of sociologists and even computer scientists, all points the same way.

We should not be discouraged by the difficulties ahead. The church is not the only institution in the early twenty-first century that has found itself at a "local maximum" and is contemplating the pitfalls of the valleys below. Take politics again, for example. The acclaimed British film director Ken Loach put the point clearly in an article for the *Independent* as he explained why he had joined hundreds of thousands of others in protest at President Bush's visit to London in 2003: "Why did I march? To give the politicians who failed me a lesson in real democracy." He is not suggesting that we get rid of our democratic political system, simply that there are other alternatives that will make democracy work better. Ways that are more interested in the exercise of education and empowerment, of peace and negotiation, than legislation and power, of regime change and war. He is talking of a democracy that works for the people on the ground rather than the fat cats in industry. As he reflects on the massively diverse group of people who gathered in agreement that the interests of the people should be put before the interests of the large corporations, he ends by saying: "I cannot recall a time when the prospects for developing that agreement into an organized grouping have been better. Can we measure up to this opportunity?"[16]

Can we measure up to this opportunity? Others are asking the same question: in education, where the fruitless practice of effecting change in schools by sending them huge folders of new policies is having to be abandoned; in economics, where the old mechanistic models of growth and recession are being overthrown by ones that talk of chaotic systems and complex networks.

Can we measure up to this opportunity? Can we as the church buck our own trends by working to change alongside other institutions, rather than twenty years behind them? I believe we can. I believe we have a unique opportunity to show how an institution that is widely acknowledged to be out of touch, is largely ignored by those it seeks to serve, and is completely detached from the blossoming interest in things spiritual, can face its fears, stop tinkering with the railroad, step down into the dark valleys, and explore completely new ways of being.

Fowler encourages us on toward a Conjunctive Church, and this book is a first attempt to sketch out what the journey might entail. It is based on the hope that we, the body of Christ, can change precisely because, in the incarnation, we see a God who has changed. Thus God has provided us with a model—perhaps not just for our own transformation but for transformation of other institutions as well.

However, I must start with a word of warning. In sketching out our search for new peaks, we must first come to terms with the fact that a map showing the position and ascent routes of Everest is simply not available to us. Like Danny Hillis, we must realize that the solutions are not going to come from hours spent preprogramming, but from the evolution of a program out of the very fundamentals of things; not from exercising our power, but from an exercise in empowerment. We cannot know what the new church is going to look like; if we could, we could construct it now. Our current consciousness cannot imagine itself into a new one. We must first descend into the valleys and let the evolutionary forces of our local situations bring a new mode of being to birth.

The final irony of Hillis's work was that, on inspecting the final miniprogram that had evolved into the Everest of number-sorting, he had absolutely no idea how it worked. What we are about to undertake may not make rational sense, and it is unlikely that we will be able to fully understand what is happening, but it is vital to our painful revival. We see in the valleys there are clouds; as we move from these comfortable peaks and seek a transformed church, we must trust ourselves to their unknowing.

Part 1.

Advent / Incarnation / Emergence

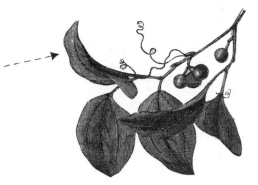

{ Advent }

. . . But before the church can change, before I can change, before anything changes, comes waiting.

A pause. A rest.

This is nature's way, decreeing as she does that movement from one direction to another cannot happen instantaneously: a zero timespan to divide the period of change would compute an infinite acceleration, requiring an infinite Force through the product of our Masses. We would be broken by it.

So against our hasty judgment, and in God's scientific wisdom, before we can experience the transformation that is vital to our survival, we will be required to wait. To be acted on gently, gracefully, and peacefully. Shaped, not crushed; guided, not dragged.

We would like change now, with immediate effect. A miracle solution. A new program that will sort everything out and make everything OK straightaway. A new meeting structure. A new building. A new method of contemplation. A course that will propel us from Stage 3 to Stage 6 in no time. We'd like to be there now, no fuss or hassle or journey or responsibility or pain. Down from the local maximum and straight up Everest. By helicopter, preferably.

Discussing the term *Emerging Church*, the Church of England report into church planting and fresh expressions of church notes that "emerging suggests an evolutionary, Spirit-led process. . . . However, the phrase may invite the existing church to play for time and wait and see what happens, rather than face the urgency of the mission task."[1] Reflecting on this, it is vital to note that the task *is* urgent, but if our response is to be anything more than another flash in the pan or botched attempt to become culturally aware, then we must avoid haste. While the church may well be "poised for serious growth and renewal,"[2] we must distinguish carefully between "waiting" and "playing for time"; the former is the proper beginning to a farsighted response, the latter a panicked delaying tactic in the face of impending crisis.

Genuine change cannot be about haste, or about playing for time. It must involve the depths of us, and must have something of us in it. There is a theory that the word *grail*, which we commonly take to mean the cup or platter Christ used at the Last Supper, historically means "gradual" and, in this sense, "the heart of the Grail Mystery is that the vessel was formed gradually through the questioning path."[3] We must realize that if we are to see real, long-lasting change, then it is going to take time; it is going to be a lifelong quest.

Our history, both ancient and modern, has been transfixed by the idea of revolution, of radical change precipitated quickly, requiring an uprising, an insurgence, a head of pressure and a focusing of force: demonstrations, coups d'état, armed struggles, wars, and regime changes. Warriors, dictators, and their critics have been clear about it for centuries. Chairman Mao Zedong wrote that "a revolution is not a dinner party. It cannot be so leisurely and gentle. . . . It is an insurrection, an act of violence by which one class overthrows another";[4] Paul Virilio in *Speed and Politics*, that "revolution will soon be entirely reduced to a permanent assault on time. The man on the battlefield has no safety other than in suicidal entrance into the very trajectory of the speed of [the guns]";[5] and Napoleon, that "the strength of a revolutionary army should be evaluated as in mechanics, by its mass multiplied by its speed." Through all their blood and violence, many of our politicians still seem to believe that these revolutions bring genuine transformation. Yet it is abundantly clear that materially, politically, psychologically, and spiritually, violent change tends to shear, to break the whole as one surface part moves and leaves the rest of the body behind unaltered.[6]

In his seminal work *Future Shock*, Alvin Toffler describes the psychological damage that occurs to people when they are overwhelmed by intense change. He talks about *future shock* being a disease of change, a sickness that people suffer that is not so much about the *direction* of change as the *rate* of it. Future shock, he says, "grows out of the increasing lag between . . . the pace of environmental change and the limited pace of human response."[7] In other words, for our own health, we need change to occur not at revolutionary speeds demanded by power-wielding dictators or company boardrooms but at the evolutionary speeds of the empowered human body.

Partly in response to Toffler's concerns, people have begun to see that the nature of change has itself been required to change. If we are to transform the whole, and truly alter the very nature of things for good, then the mode of change cannot be *revolution*, but *evolution*. A gradual development over a long period of time. As Robert Warren notes, "A good case can be made for evolution being the best single word summary of an Anglican approach to change. It suggests creativity [and] responsiveness to present environment."[8]

The slowness of evolution certainly has a divine beauty about it with its gentle, unseen transformation so hard to plot yet so undeniable in its force. We would like change with immediate effect—we want revolution—but God's ways are not our ways and God's thoughts are higher than ours. Despite this, as we will see in the next chapter, we have projected our revolutionary tendencies onto God, and it is only as revelation has become clearer over time that we have seen that ours is not a God of violent uprising but of slow, slow evolution. So since forever, and until whenever, those who have sought to change God's way have had to endure a prefix of . . .

Waiting

As Sarah waited—90 years for a son to fulfill God's
  promise
We wait in hope for what we thought had been spoken to us

As Moses waited—40 years in the desert
We wait for emptiness and humility

As the Prophets waited—1000 years of salvation
  promises
We wait for signs of presence

As Mary waited—9 months of her 14 years for the
  child of God
We feel the birth-pains, yet fear for the child

As John the Baptist waited—scanning the crowds
  for knowing eyes
We long for an experience of the Divine

As Christ waited—30 years of creeping time
40 days in the throes of temptation
3 years in the midst of misunderstanding
3 days in the depths of hell . . .

So now, we wait.
Our turn to toil on levelling mountains and straight-
    ening paths
Our turn to watch time's horizon
Our turn to hope that he who promised is faithful,
    and will return.[9]

Before the church can change, before I can change, before things change—before change, we must wait. Caught "between the now and the not yet," the set on which we now take our short parts front-stage, and the plot up to this point, all heave with people and peoples forced to accept God's immaculate restraint in holding back the full force of immediacy. The cast has thronged with the silent parts of those given to not receive, to not see, to not make it, to not hear, to not be freed, to not understand, to wait, wait, wait for something, someone, some sign, some change, some hint not yet hinted at, some word not yet spoken, some dream not yet interpreted, some revival not yet . . . yet . . . Yet they did not give in. Their still waiting bones lie as dry and fertile testaments to their faith in that which they did not see come to pass. Climbing on their shoulders, we now search concrete horizons for some thing, some perception, some movement, and have to do so without timetables or schedules or LED displays or countdown timers. Stripped of our usual support mechanisms and technical augurs, we wait for the one who whispers, "Behold, I am doing a new thing . . . Do you not perceive it?" (Isa. 43:19 RSV).

Only if I am still. Only if I have stopped what I was doing to listen and hold my breath and enter some spiritual apnea

45

and wait. The perception of the new step will come only to those brave enough to stop dancing the old. The realization that we must descend this low peak will come only to those prepared to stop and take stock of their position. We fear that if we stopped for a week, a month, a service, a moment, we might be forgotten, or lose our momentum, weaken our profile, appear ill-thought-out and failing. So we feed the ecclesiastic furnaces our burned-out wrecks: tired leaders, disillusioned ministers, fatigued congregations—marshalling them to dance longer, march faster, pray harder, cry louder in earnest for God to come, come, COME and batter our hearts into change. (While Elijah waits.)

We must be brave enough to stop if we are to see change. "Sabbath was made for man, not man for the Sabbath" (Mark 2:27). In other words, "Our structures must serve us, not us serve them." This is the vital truth that the owners of the railroad missed. The only way to consider whether our structures are serving us is to stop and reflect on them. To dismantle them; take them apart piece by piece. Expose them to the air. Lay them on the ground and let everyone walk around them and get a good look at them without the pressures of meetings and deadlines and agendas. This is the beginning of empowerment: we must allow people space and time to return to the deep simplicity of things, and spend time mulling over the fundamentals, the nuts and bolts that interlock to make our complex lives.

To stop people in their tracks, to stop yourself, and suggest that the way to higher peaks is actually to return to the valleys, is a brave act of true leadership. It is an admission that the way we have been—the road we have been traveling—has reached a dead end; it is thus a daring statement renouncing power, and declaring that leadership will no longer exercise it, but will serve by empowering.

This is a dangerous invitation for newness, carrying the risk that those we give such freedom to might freely walk away, or freely imagine something better than we had. But freedom must be what we are about. So the truly free, the brave who truly seek God, will always have periods, commas, full stops, punctuation marks, pregnant pauses, breves and semibreves of silence where those around them are given the freedom to walk; given space to deconstruct structures, to reimagine and rethink. Blue-sky thinking cannot happen while we rush around under thunderclouds of busyness. "We must bear fruit," Christ tells us. But outside our genetically modified, globalized supermarkets, fruit trees only bear fruit once a year and then their branches are stripped of leaves in the cold winter of advent.

It is difficult to write about waiting; we turn from Malachi to Matthew without a thought. But perhaps between the testaments God symbolically stopped, brought down the curtain on another act as he had done with the Flood, with forty years in the desert, and with the exile in 587 BC. We read from Matthew 1:24 to Matthew 1:25 with no pause for breath, when perhaps we should also symbolically stop, hold our breath, and consider the unwritten wait—what of Mary's nine months of pregnancy? How did she feel? Excluded? Rejected? Shunned? Frightened? Excited? We simply do not know. All we do know is that she descended the small peak of her simple girlhood into the valley and clouds of unknowing, the mystery of her faith apparent in her certainty of the higher peaks she could not yet see. Perhaps we should insert blank pages between these unpaginated moments, pages we would have to turn so that our thoughts might turn too and consider these punctuation marks, where God stops and waits before birthing something new.

Of course, in many ways the church is destined to live in a perpetual advent as we wait for Christ's return. But within that grand scheme, it seems that at the start of this new century we are also living in a particular advent, that we are being called to wait for new birth again. We have already seen that we cannot at this point know what the church that will emerge will look like, just as we cannot tell from an embryo what features it will have when full-grown. To try to preempt and predetermine these features would smack of the impatience of revolution. No matter how impatient we get as a society, with processing speeds rising and our whole cultural velocity increasing ever faster, we cannot speed up pregnancy. We still have to wait the same patient nine months that Mary did, not knowing, not seeing, not being able to hurry things along. In this advent that we find ourselves in, between the "modern" church that was and is dying, and the emerging church that is not yet, we must exercise patience. We must descend into the cloud of unknowing. We must stop and wait.

Forgive me if it seems we are forever stepping back. We know we need to change, but how to? And now we know we must first wait, but how to? In a church and society so enamored with power and action, the act of doing nothing and being forced to wait is anathema, but it is essential.

Waiting can be experienced as a total loss of power: having to be in another's control, reliant on them to arrive, to act, to turn up, and all we can do is sit and wait and make ourselves comfortable. There are rare occasions when we are forced into this position—a car broken down in the middle of the highway—times when we really can do nothing, and in these resigned spaces a strange peace often comes over us.

Yet more often than not, we fool ourselves that we can take control, that some small chink of power still remains, which balloons like our blood pressure and finds us up and straining, calling road service, checking watches, listening to traffic reports, seeking explanations, and demanding attention . . . None of which will likely hurry that which we wait for, but all of which will bolster our façade of control, of feeling useful, of power.

Somewhere between the freedom of being able to do nothing, and the pretense of having to do something, is the sort of mysterious waiting of the saints and the prophets—a combination of catharsis and contemplation, of clearing the decks for the new, while being content to exist in unknowing. As we wait for the kingdom to break through again now, we are not called to inaction, to do nothing but lie back and wait for glory. But neither are we called to frenzied activity, which will leave no space for newness to be sown and grown. We must have the courage to stop. To prepare the ground for the new, and wait.

In his book *Hopeful Imagination*, theologian Walter Brueggemann explores the different ways that the prophets Jeremiah, Ezekiel, and Isaiah helped the people of Israel to deal with their movement down from a local maximum into exile. Introducing the main thrust of the book, he writes:

> This [prophetic] literature is from a period when the known world of Jerusalem was destroyed in 587 BC and with it the props and symbols which held life together. . . . [These prophets] are cast in the difficult role of providing voice and articulation to the faith and experience of a community in exile. Their pastoral responsibility was to help people *enter into* exile, be in exile and *depart out* of exile . . . to help them relinquish the old world, and receive the new.[10]

He goes on to add that he believes that

> the reception of a new world from God is under way in our time. It is apparent in the staggering, frightening emergence of new communities . . . dangerous emergences are paralleled by dreams of justice and mercy in our culture that dare to affirm that old structures may be transformed to be vehicles for the new gifts of God. Thus we are at the risky point of receiving from God what we thought God would not give, namely a new way to be human in the world.[11]

49

Nearly twenty years after these words were written, perhaps they are beginning to find their resonance as we experience more and more vividly the dismantling of the "props and symbols" and "old structures" which have made up our known world in the Stage 3 Church for so long. Alongside so many large institutions, the church is heading for its own version of 587 BC (when Jerusalem was sacked and the Israelites were taken into exile). A time of exile—of having to stop and wait—is upon us, and we must go through this exile if we are to receive from God "a new way to be human in the world."

The movement into exile is a movement into Fowler's Stage 4. It is a movement into the valleys, into the dark night of the soul, into an absence, into a non-space where the external authorities that we relied on for security and meaning have been deconstructed and are no longer. It is painful, but it is a pain necessary for our development: leaving home, moving to a new house, marriage—all have necessary moments of exile in their respective journeys. Israel had to face this pain. Whether God had abandoned them, or they had abandoned God, was just semantics. What mattered was how they responded. Similarly for us now, the arguments about whether we have drifted or God has drifted ahead of us are irrelevant—what is patently clear is that the church is experiencing separation, delamination, marginalization, trivialization, and exile from the world it seeks to serve. And it is therefore experiencing these things from God too, for if the church is not connected to its host culture and society, it is not where God wants it to be, and therefore not where God is. "If the Church is not missionary, it has denied its calling, for it has departed from the very nature of God."[12]

We could, of course, listen to these prophets' contemporaries who "dress the wound of my people as though it were not serious," saying "'peace, peace' . . . when there

50

is no peace" (Jer. 6.14). But to do so would be foolish, for if God is doing a new thing, we *must* apply ourselves to perceiving it or risk becoming custodians of empty stone buildings and historical curiosities ourselves. Like those sleeping in comfort on the *Titanic*, we must open ourselves not only to the possibility of exile but also to its imminent necessity. We must not be foolish and simply jump ship in desperation and resignation. We must think through the instructions that have been left us for surviving the darkness we are about to sail into. We must brace ourselves properly for the return to the valleys below. I believe that Brueggemann's exposition of the way the prophets helped Israel cope with their exile is excellent preparation for us too.[13]

"Only grief permits newness"

Brueggemann draws from the writings of Jeremiah that the first step through the journey of exile, or the first stage of the waiting process as I am calling it, is grief.[14] Indeed, he surmises that *only* through grief can newness become a possibility.

In his poetry, Jeremiah is encouraged by God to help the people to truly feel and accept his absence. Jerusalem has been sacked. All has been destroyed. They have been exiled and their concept of God vaporized. All has been lost. But rather than attempt a stiff upper lip, a façade of "it's OK," Jeremiah encourages full and honest acceptance of the facts as they are. There must be no denial, no clinging to the dead or harking back to a past now destroyed. Instead they must open their arms, release their grips, throw back their heads and feel the emptiness, feel the absence, feel the defeat and weep, weep, weep for their loss. This honest grieving is the required first step of the exile. Without it there can be no newness, for we are left still clinging to that which is past and dead, unable to grasp the new.

There is a spectacular lack of grief in our churches today. The texts of so many Christian magazines, sermons, and songs are all woven into an enormous blanket of denial that we wrap warmly around us, smothering the honest doubts with an ever-optimistic hue of "everything is good, and God is with us." Hands are raised, but never to ask questions, only in surrender to programs of services, outreaches, prayer meetings, and worship. Eyes are shut, less blinded by glory as blind to the facts that numbers are falling, churches are closing, the "revival" didn't come, society is losing interest, and our circle of influence is decreasing.

Christ invited us to this work, declaring that in his Father's house were many rooms . . . But we grasp his words at face value and take his free board and lodgings in the plentiful rooms he has prepared for us. We settle ourselves and add our comforts, and putter, while he waits for us to join him outside. And we meet at conferences and nod and agree that this is the right thing to do. And we dress up in our strange finery and ink out carefully crafted statements that we stick on our notice boards and nod again and agree that this is what we should do. Like kleptomaniac recluses, we have burrowed our way deep into our little obsessions, creating labyrinthine corridors that prevent much natural light getting in, their intricate and strange comforts leaving us to wander them for years without ever stepping outside as we grow increasingly suspicious of the world that points and laughs at our peeling frames and overgrown garden.

There is no grief in this cheerless house. Where are the tears? Where are the honest appraisals? Where is the daring speech that admits we have reached a low peak and must now head down? "If my people don't speak," Christ said, "even the stones would cry out"—and because we don't, the stones now do, grieving alone in the empty spaces

52

they enclose, weeping damp tears because we seem unable. As the Church of England report *Mission-Shaped Church* advises, "This is a moment for repentance. We have allowed our culture and the Church to drift apart."[15] Grief and repentance are the proper antidote for the culture of denial and cover-up that has so permeated our church and wider society. Denial is born where we fear the future—fear the consequences of admitting the light of truth into our murky fictions, afraid that we might be seen as failures. We ought to find truth each Sunday; instead we go for doses of fiction, enough to cloud our perception for the week ahead that everything is OK. Not that we only suffer this in church. We are surrounded by ungrieving politicians, all of whom confidently assure us they are going to lead their parties to victory; ungrieving CEOs, unable to admit poor performance lest they lose their grip on valuable share options. Indeed, it seems we live most of our lives bathed in the dark light of façade, unable to grieve, told to soldier on with stiff upper lips, denying everything, building up a nice head of grief-repressed pressure before we have it all out under the knife of a bypass surgeon or on the couch of a shrink.

Where are the truly independent media that will speak the truth and give permission and uncritical space for grief? Where are the Jeremiahs today who will help the church to face its loss and grieve? Like Jeremiah, they will be found on the edges. In the side or back pews. They are the artists and satirists, whose very nature is to hold up a mirror and show us our true face. They are the powerless, who have no vested interest in keeping the present system propped up. They are the scarred, who know too much about pain to shy away from the honest truth. They are those who claim not to know "how to speak," for they are only children (Jer. 1:6). We know them. They are at Stage 4. They are on our edges, and it is the responsibility of those of us at the center to make room for their difficult message before they leave unheard. They are vital to us, for stopping and grieving will be most difficult for those of us who have had most to gain from this crumbling regime. But we must do it, we must stop all the programs, stop the meetings, stop the denials, stop the machinations, dismantle the structures, face our fears and disappointments, and weep for the absence, weep for the emptiness, weep for the pretense, weep for the fiction. Weep until we can see our barrenness clearly, for only then will we have made room for newness.

"Only holiness brings hope"

Once we have grieved, our tear-washed eyes can then properly open to the shocking fact that God allowed this to happen. God allowed us to climb this little peak. The denial may be over, and the cover-ups exposed, but a deeper resistance still remains. How could God do this? In the midst of our waiting for the new, we meet this intractable issue: if we are seeking the new, then what we were practicing was the old, and therefore God was not in what we were doing anymore. God has moved on back down the mountain while we stayed up on our comfortable hillock.

Such a divine departure is rightly shocking to us. We see an example of it described in Ezekiel 10: God ups and leaves the temple. To a people who had become overfamiliar and blasé about God's presence with them in the temple, to a people who had become complacent about their special status as the Chosen, God showed God's holiness. God got up and left. Bored by our rambling, navel-gazing conversation about internal tinkering, God hung up. God walked off—displaying a true, holy freedom that shouts clearly over its shoulder that "no temple, no place, no people, no box, no church, no agenda, no theological position will ever require *me* to stay where I don't want, be co-opted into something I only half agree with, be pressed into the service of some cause you made up because I AM who I AM." And, SLAM, the door shuts and we are left alone to wonder about God's holiness, God's transcendence, God's otherness, God's separateness, God's difference.

As we enter this dangerous place of stopping and waiting, we must face the possibility of experiencing God's disinterest. Where we have proclaimed "God is in this," we must be prepared to admit that God can and does leave. One need only consider for a second the other pole where God was *un*able to leave any ministry, any place, any attempt at work, and see that it would quickly draw us down the same path to the god who, not being allowed to permit suffering, intervened every time a child stepped toward a sharp object.

God will not be co-opted into our programs. And this actually turns out to be the foundation of huge hope. For if God could not leave, then we would be bound and trapped forever inside structures that God "might just be blessing." How many times have we squirmed at some toe-curling "ministry" yet been snared to our seats by the mantra that "if God touches just one person one tiny amount through this, then it's worth it"? Enough of this pseudo-spiritual bull. God's holiness gives hope beyond this otherwise perpetual trap of "what if?" and "perhaps."

To admit that God can and will leave is to allow the dangerous taste of hope into otherwise stagnant waters. It is to admit that the life of the disciple is not sedentary but nomadic—moving on to where sustenance lies, not staying where sustenance once was. It is to appreciate that the journey of faith is not a static conversion but an evolution of the Spirit. The very fact that God can move on means that hope is possible. That we are not stuck with what we have. That this *isn't* it. God has to move from us, out of sight into the deep horizon, down into the clouds, holy and loving. Urging us to follow, but refusing to stay. "I opened for my lover, but my lover had left; he was gone. My heart sank at his departure. I looked for him but did not find him. I called him but he did not answer" (Song of Songs 5:6). To admit God's holy freedom is to acknowledge that true love will never demand union, that it must move and shift and pull and push and hold and release and always set free, and be present in absent yearning as much as in intercourse.

"Only memory allows possibility"

From Sarah's barren wait to Christ's embryonic advent, God teaches us that change comes through evolution, not revolution. That time must be taken. That we must stop, wait, and face up to where we are. That if we are to see change that is transformative rather than tactical, we must open our fists, relinquish the old, and learn to live with emptiness. Grieve. Admit God's freedom and draw hope. The structures have been deconstructed, the plot cleared. Now we must wait and wonder wherefrom newness will come.

From the writings of the second part of Isaiah, Brueggemann speculates that only through the practice of memory will new possibility emerge.

Without some form of memory, this sentence you are reading or hearing would make no sense. It is only our ability to hold the however-recent past in mind and bring it to bear on our present that allows us to learn, to advance, to understand, to converse, to relate in depth, to love. To move forward from nothing into something.

Without memory we become imprisoned in an absolute present, unaware of the direction we have come from, and therefore what direction we are heading in. Without memory there can be no momentum, no discernible passage of time, and therefore no movement or velocity: we become stuck in the way things are with no options, unable to appreciate that things might have been different in the past and therefore can be in the future.

As the Israelites in exile began to accept their lot as their Babylonian captors fed it to them, Isaiah stepped in and began to exercise their imaginations. His poetry opened the sealed vaults of their minds and forced them to recover their collective memory. By allowing the memories of how God had worked through them in the past to be resurrected, he simultaneously reinvigorated their imaginations, thereby inspiring new thoughts and possibilities.

Our problem today: the space for imagination to expand and take shape is inversely proportional to the speed at which we live. Driven hard and fast, we lack the time to allow alternate worlds and possibilities to form, careening past small turnings and exits, bound to follow the obvious straight paths of the present arrangement. Yet if we stop and wait, and close our eyes to the "buy now, take me now" images, and rest our weary retinas, we will begin to remember, new worlds will form, new exits will become apparent. Only the exercise of memory will allow this possibility.

Before the church can change, before I can change, before things change—before change, comes waiting. A pause. A rest. What is stopping that new world forming? Who is saying "no"? Who is saying "impossible"? Only those whose interest lies in keeping things as they are now: those with power and interest (in)vested.

We must not worry about them. We must stop. Wait. Allow ourselves to grieve. Meditate on God's freedom and absence. Begin to dream where God might now like to be found. Not in the house, but in a stable; not in Jerusalem, but from Nazareth; not with his family, but in the temple; not in the temple, but with the sick, the poor, the disinterested, the ordinary, the real, the drinkers, smokers, jokers, deviators, and slackers . . . In some new post-Enlightenment place we never thought possible, God still lingers, waiting to be born.

------2.

{ Incarnation }

Caesarean Sections

From Caesar, a census
Grim counting and recording
He rationalises all he has fought over.
From God, a song,
Divine harmony from angels uncountable
An irrational freedom and declaration of peace,
    while . . .

Herod, the puppet king
His opulent palace, sick with fear
Echoing with insecurity and desperation at
Christ the true king
His pungent bed and mother's arms sick with fear
Swaying with insecurity and desperation as
1000 mothers scream and 1000 innocents die.
This puppet flailing and the death throes of
    destruction

Cutting down young life in fear that
A young life will cut him down,
   while . . .

In the temple, the priests declare peace
That all is settled.
That God has assured them of their place.
So they take their places at overloaded tables
Too comfortable to crane necks at wandering stars
   and
Too settled for chilly hillsides.
But God is unsettled
Uncomfortable in this petrified home
And slips away unnoticed through the curtain,
   while . . .

The bitter old man stands at the gates of the earth
Waiting
Watching
Guarding the only entrance and exit to this citadel
   planet.
The babies file in and the dead file out
And he watches them

Grimly keeping count.
He watches
He waits
He shivers to shake
The tired cold from his limbs
For he must stay awake
For the one they say will attempt a salvation.
He keeps one eye on the horizon
On the distant reaches of the future
Wherefrom surely his nemesis will ride with
   armies
And demand entry:
The battle of the gates of the earth

So heighten awareness and tighten security and
all the while . . .

He does not notice the infant God
Slipping in among the embryonic ranks
Of those awaiting entry.
Become powerless
To slip the trap of the powerful.
A Trojan baby
Now inside the citadel planet.
Waiting, hiding, growing
Evolving an inner salvation
(The original subversion)[1]

Having waited, waited, waited for so long, the anticipation
building, the hype and rumor and false Messiahs, and all
the while things getting worse with occupations and pu-
nitive taxations and military machinations—some giving
up hope and some transferring it to others, and others
philosophizing it into abstraction while still others distill
it into direct action . . . Into all this chaos Christ slipped
virtually unnoticed. How else did we expect God to enter
the world?

In his book *God: A Biography*, Jack Miles portrays the
God of the Old Testament as an adolescent, unsure of his
place or how best to wield his powers, a divinity growing
up as the testament unfolded. It is as if God was actually going through Fowler's stages, beginning with the
crude interactions and incarnations of Stages 1 and 2,
and evolving into a self-confident, young adult divinity
at Stage 3. Of course one could equally argue that it is
simply *our* understanding of God that has matured, and
that as generations have spent more time immersed in this
relationship, we have begun to see God in more subtle
ways than simple creation and destruction, fertility and
barrenness.

61

Perhaps this explains how the Old Testament can show us a God of inclusion, grace, compassion, and mercy alongside a God who appears to desire lands plundered, cities pillaged, and peoples slaughtered: it is a story of our getting to know God and our maturing spirituality, rather than of God getting to know us and God growing up. So our Bible has our failings and bright perceptions recorded side by side—the penetrating insights of Isaiah 53 and the nationalistic, divine co-option of Joshua 8—not as precedents for us to copy in ignorance, but reminders of where the journey has taken us.

Looking at it from this viewpoint, one can imagine God's frustration in trying to communicate with the people of the Old Testament. Having to channel messages through the ranks of priests and scribes and judges led to a kind of divine Chinese whispers, with layer upon layer of interpretation and translation and subtle personal agenda being carefully added until the original truth was almost completely occluded from the people it was meant for.

We see Christ venting his Father's irritation at this ciphering of meaning when he chastises the religious leaders of the day in Matthew 23 for being "blind guides"—as if referring to the metaphorical local peaks that they had led the people up and now refused to move from. He went on to lament the way they killed all the prophets sent to them "from Abel to Zechariah," and then told those gathered in the temple "the parable of the tenants": when the landowner had sent his servants and they had been beaten, killed, and stoned, he had to resort to sending them his son in the hope that they would listen to him.

God understood that the only way to communicate his character truthfully and without distortion was to bypass the intermediaries, the interlocutors, and to speak to us himself. The experiment involving trickle-down truth had been shown to be totally ineffective, with those higher up the pyramid co-opting and distorting for their own selfish gain, leaving God caricatured as an angry, malevolent revolutionary who demanded regular sacrifice to appease his wrath; a God with a nationalistic interest who would support the Jewish people come what may. God had to put this right.

And so as we turn from Malachi to Matthew, those four hundred quiet years reduced to a single leaf of Bible paper, it is as if we are seeing Jack Miles's teenage God, so rampant and delinquent in his rough diamond youth, born again an immediately more mature and mellowed figure: a Stage 3 God who has gone through the intertestamental darkness of Stage 4 and been reborn at Stage 5. Or to read the same apparent maturing the other way: in those four hundred years God withdrew and said nothing.[2] It was we who had to experience movement between the stages. We waited and grieved, our Old Testament closed and finished in a metaphorical death and silence. It was a cooling-off period, if you will; a chance for us to reflect and break clean from the old, so that when Christ came we were able to see this reborn God afresh from a new angle—a God of compassion and wisdom and grace and nonviolent force and loving holiness . . . Not that God had not been these things before, but in our angst-ridden immaturity and tribal insecurity, we had distorted them as we strained to see from our little peaks, projecting them imperfectly onto warped screens, and co-opting their distorted images of a revolutionary God for our own uses.

We still do. We dress Christ as Che Guevara and take up our swords to do battle against Darwins and Galileos, and in doing so put on again the old masks of an embattled, violent, and intolerant God. If only we would look beyond our immature projections and egocentric worldviews and contemplate what has been revealed to us, we would see that, rather than being locked into stony immutability, God has been evolving, adapting, and decentralizing since space/time began. Perhaps God's own progress has not been so different from that of the "big bang"—a huge, centralized mass of energy and matter exploding, expanding, and creating. Not losing energy but rather transforming it into light and work and heat, God's entropy and order ever dispersing and widening its reach.

God saw that the only way out of this Old Testament misconception and misrepresentation was to forget the trickle-down, top-down system of communication and to disappear for a while. God could not immediately begin something new, but had to wait, be silent, and metaphorically die before re-emerging. Rather than shout down to us from the top of Everest, God would climb down into the valleys below and join us, a reborn God now inside the system—an "incarnate" being in the same body as us, one of us and therefore able to speak to us unmediated in our own language and idiom.

Totally within character, God saw what needed to be done, took the plunge, and became nothing. He stripped away all power, might, knowledge, glory, metaphysicality—all that could obviously signify divinity was ripped out, all preconceived ideas of God-ness were discarded and torn from him. His self was refined and reduced down and down to pure essence, to the smallest possible format with no more than the most fundamental resources, to the very basics of unadorned life: a single sperm with only enough strength to breach the walls of an ovum.

Having waited, waited, waited for so long for God to come to us, what did we expect? A marching army? A blinding flash of divine lightning, striking the wicked and raising up the righteous, graves a-cracking and trumpets sounding?

Think again, God says.

64

Think again.

Free your minds from the old.

Empty them.

"I am doing a new thing. Do you not perceive it?"

The God who created evolution and dreamt up emergence knew the only door into this world was through birth to a woman. God knew that the only way to overcome the crisis of representation and communication was to give up on the top-down approach that demanded change by revolution, and be reborn, to re-emerge and change things by evolution from the bottom up.

> Through torn sky shepherds spy heaven singing
> and through this wound, God falls into hay
>   screaming.
> Only astrologers scan outer depths to follow this
>   bright trajectory
> Burning up in my atmospheres.
> Cold vacuums resisting God's re-entry.[3]

The church now seems to stand in the same place as God stood in some 2,500 years ago: misrepresented, accused of bigotry, portrayed as narrow-minded and in love with power, only interested in buildings, ready to smite the dirty and sinful, over-occupied with sex, and ready to lend support for unjust wars . . . And so we must do as God did, as Christ commanded and exemplified: we must be born again. Become nothing, removed of strength and power and voice and means and language.

We must re-emerge and grow up again in the place we are meant to serve. Understand it, learn from it, be in it, love it, listen to it, wait thirty years before speaking to it. We must, like God, discard any thoughts that revolution is going to effect change in the church or our world, and become dedicated to change by evolution.

This dedication to change by evolution flies in the face of much of our theology, politics, and policy. "The only way to save the village," they said in Vietnam, "was to destroy it." And now we say, "The only way to protect ourselves from violence is to wage a war of shock and awe on terror." And part of our hearts expects God to toe this line . . . and we have to admit that part of us wishes God had. We wish that Christ's coming had been all drama and astonishment, making it perfectly clear who was boss and leaving no room for doubt. Precisely. No room for doubt and no room for belief. No room for choice and no room for relationship. Those looking for God to do "regime change" are again projecting and co-opting like Joshua. They are stuck at Stage 3. They are people who have forgotten how to wait. They have forgotten the miracle of restraint, have become blind to the divine understanding that revolution changes nothing but the flag. Only evolution changes the genes, the whole person, the spirit—but it takes time and requires patience.

At the end of his moving book of reflections on 9/11, Rowan Williams meditates on why he titled the book *Writing in the Dust*. Having thought about the overpowering dust in the atmosphere he experienced for himself that day, and the transient nature of words written in dust, he reflects on how the story in John 8 of the woman taken in adultery spoke to him:

> When the accusation is made, Jesus at first makes no reply but writes with his finger on the ground. What on earth is he doing? Commentators have had plenty of suggestions, but there is one meaning that seems to me obvious in the light of what I think we learned that morning [of September 11]. He hesitates. He does not draw a line, fix an interpretation, tell the woman who she is and what her fate should be. He allows a moment, in which people are given time to

see themselves differently precisely because he refuses to make the sense they want. When he lifts his head, there is both judgement and release.

So this is writing in the dust because it tries to hold that moment for a little longer, long enough for some of our demons to walk away.[4]

God continues to "write in the dust," refusing to offer immediate solutions and pronounce hasty judgments. God waits, holds moments, and refuses to fix interpretations or draw hard lines. God does it to force us from the mind-set of revolutionary immediacy—a mind-set that gives swift birth to violent counterattack and retaliation—into the mind-set of measured evolution, whereby our demons slink away as we wait for newness to grow, not listening to their mob-cry for newness to be ripped from the belly of the old.

As we wonder how the church could change, I have suggested that we must begin by waiting. Second, I am going to suggest that, like God, we must be born again. That we must re-emerge. That there will be no revolution, only evolution. That what will be in the future body of Christ must be what Christ was: the embryonic cooperation of divinity and humanity.

This is the mystery of the incarnation: that Christ was both fully God and fully human, and his very birth sums up what we must do. He came into this world invisible to the human eye, beneath the radar of the authorities, undetected by those blinded by power. And now we, like Mary, need to become wombs of the divine, allowing God to fertilize our creativity and give birth to newness. But even in that birthing we must be aware of our expectations. The newness that will be born will be incomplete and immature. It will be newness not fully formed and unable to speak. It will be newness defenseless and unable to justify itself to its seniors. It will be newness that is born into a culture and therefore totally and naturally immersed in the codes, the language, the history and life of that which it comes to serve.

Too often we kill off new ideas and inspirations before they can really take root—a fact observed by Christ in the parable of the sower. We often expose new growth too quickly to the full force of the sun, leaving it "hung out to dry" and at great risk of burning out by expecting too much of it too soon before secure roots are put down. I have seen many cases of people with "great testimonies" put on pedestals and thrown into the spotlight to witness, only to feel the heat and wither away. The other danger is of surrounding new growth with too much to battle against—requiring it to justify its existence in the face of other stronger organisms at endless meetings. We must be aware that those with inspiration will not immediately be able to rationalize their ideas to questioning leaders keen to see that everything fits into "the vision." Often when the inspired are forced to closely define their vision, their energy is sapped, and they too wither away.

We must stop and wait, and allow newness to emerge among us. And when it does we must treat it just as Mary did Christ, just as we would any other newborn. We must nurture it gently and feed it carefully. We must not demand it act like an adult, but allow it to be a child. We must understand again that new growth will take a long time and will require a lot of long-term support. There are no speedy revolutions in the process of gestation and development; only slow, sure, stable growth.

If we are to become wombs of the divine, then what we give birth to will not only take a great deal of careful nurturing but will also be very specific to the culture and place where it is born. In order to reach humanity, God had to re-emerge and be reborn into human form. In the same way, we need to re-emerge and be reborn into specific places and cultures in order to be truly incarnate to them and so to reach them. God came all the way to us—yet we now expect people to come so far toward us in church. Far away from their music, far away from their vernacular, far away from their visual language, their codes and symbols. God was born again—became nothing and re-emerged—in order to reach us in our own language, to live and grow up among us. As the body of Christ, we must do likewise and, just as for Christ, this re-emerging will take immense courage.

On the other hand it will take no courage to sit at the comfortable tables of the priests, and no courage to do surveys and censuses. The rational minds will carry on counting their riches and the professional religious will continue to be cushioned by enthusiasts. The quiet force of God's evolution will not be detected by those looking for revival or those demanding reformation, for the embryonic is only detectable by ultrasound, beyond the range of normal hearing. But out on cold hillsides and in far-off cities there are laborers and stargazers who have the courage to imagine that newness is not only possible but inevitable. It is growing in the belly of a young girl with no power or money. It is feeding on the life of one condemned as immoral by the religious and excluded by her community. It exists in the hopeful yearnings of old prophets, promised by God that they will see new life, and in the faith of the mothers who have been declared barren. It is seen most clearly by those with no power to lose, and its direction is revealed to those prepared to search the heavens and remain unimpressed with the powerful.

Christ's incarnation is a magnificent source of hope for the hopeless, for out of silence, out of the cold night, out of the dark valley, out of nothing, something new and extraordinary appears. In these times when we desperately need newness, we need to hold on to God's ability to evolve and adapt and ground our hope there, even as we wait in apparent darkness, unable to predict the form that that newness could take.

The Great Reversal

Walking with the crowds
Carried along by the pressing forward.
Each one eager to get ahead
But each one starting the same:
Born as a baby, and from then on, struggling towards
    meaning, power and influence.
Be someone
Be remembered
Make a big impression.
Leave some indelible mark in your 3 score years
    and 10.

From birth, a struggle to find eternity, to burst
    through life with such dazzling intensity, that
    everyone will remember forever.
But walking the other way, picking out a route
    against the crowds, a solitary figure passes me . . .
    passes all of us—all straining away innocence, to
    be someone,
And he passes us, a quiet chaos in the crowd.

Christ, eternal, omniscient, creator, beyond time,
    source of wisdom and beyond petty claims of
    influence . . . in very nature God, slips into reverse
    and walks back past us—away from Kingship,
    away from power, away from influence, away from
    eternity, away from wisdom . . . towards infancy.
Calmly stepping into the body of a tiny child.

And even as this baby grows, figuring out how to con-
    trol the body he himself designed, he still walks the

other way, realising that life cannot be found in the struggle for permanence, but in giving it up.

This Great Reversal subverts me. Tired of pressing forward, I realise I need to turn, for what I have been searching for has just walked past me the other way.[5]

-------3.

{ Emergence }

Christ's emergence as a baby, born into a specific culture and a particular time, is an archetype for change. We must stop. Wait. Allow God God's freedom and let the old pass away. Free our memories and open our imaginations to be impregnated; become wombs of the divine and give birth to newness in our particular place and time.

Christ's incarnation in a specific time and a specific place demands of us, the body of Christ, that we too undergo incarnation and are born somewhere specific, committing to it and putting roots down. We cannot be reborn in first-century Palestine; we need to be incarnate to the place where we are and the place that most needs us. We must learn how to incarnate the church in the city.

Becoming incarnate will mean the same for us as it did Christ. We will have to experience being small and defenseless, requiring nurture from our host world just as Christ needed Mary's milk. We cannot and must not remain rootless people or rootless churches. Christ needed water from the earth, food from the ground, education from his elders; yet we too often experience church as an organization that has absolutely no need for its surrounding community or area. It is too often an appendage, something slightly apart and independent, not needing the neighboring culture in order to survive. To admit our need as a church, our dependence on our host culture, is a risk. Yet like Christ we must take this risk of interdependence, this risk of being born, this risk of life.

We must be born again. We must re-emerge into our communities as infants. We must stop, wait, imagine, remember. Become wombs of the divine and undergo reincarnation in the very places we live. And Christ's experience tells us that if we are going to minister to these communities, to speak to them in languages they will understand, to represent God without distortion, then we will have to understand thoroughly how these local places work. For it is only once we understand how our host culture works from the inside that we will even begin to understand what an emerging church dedicated to serving that host culture might look like.

Throughout every continent, there has been a dramatic shift in the way people are living together. In 1900, only 14 percent of humanity lived in cities. By 2000, 47 percent did, and now, into 2007, we have reached the tipping point: over half of the world's population live in cities. Even for those of us who live in suburban or rural areas, our lives are very often affected by the powerful fields of influence that cities throw off. Yet our models of church have not kept up with this radical change. It is my belief that if we are to reincarnate the church in our locality—wherever that may be—we must engage with the far-reaching impacts of this global urbanization. So, toward this goal of understanding our host cultures, and in particular the cities that an increasing number of us live in or are influenced by, I want to explore some of the principles of city life, and in particular the ways in which cities can be seen to display "emergent" properties. I believe that if the body of Christ is going to become conjunctive and be incarnate in the emergent community, then it will need to become emergent itself. To do this, we need to first understand something of the science of emergence.

In a chapter entitled "The Kind of Problem a City Is," Jane Jacobs wrote in her classic critique of urban planning *The Death and Life of Great American Cities* of the three basic sorts of problems that science has had to deal with. First, from the seventeenth to the nineteenth century, scientists learned how to analyze problems of simplicity, where one quantity—say, gas pressure—depends primarily on a second quantity—say, gas volume. Second, in the period after 1900, scientists jumped from such "two-variable" problems to learn to deal with multimillion-variable problems through statistical analysis. It is only recently that the gap between problems with very small and very large numbers of variables has been able to be plugged. Such problems, with half a dozen or even several dozen quantities varying simultaneously in interconnected ways, have been termed *organized complexity*, and this is the sort of "problem" Jacobs concludes a city is. Thus the cities we live in, around, and are influenced by, like many "organized complexity" situations, have numbers of variables that are "interrelated into an organic whole,"[1] and it is this interrelated, many-variable, evolving kind of system that has been termed *emergent*.

In his excellent book *Emergence*, Steven Johnson began reflecting on this analysis of the urban situation by looking at two other complicated "organisms" that displayed emergent properties: the human brain and an ant colony. At first sight an ant colony, like a city, appears to be completely anarchic. A huge mass scurrying in different directions, every body seemingly oblivious to the others. All in a hurry to carry out some task and clambering over one another in desperation to complete it. Yet closer inspection reveals a high level of order. Some ants are collecting food, while others are disposing of waste. Still others are carrying the bodies of dead comrades out to the "burial ground" of the colony.

So who decides the positions of these burial and waste grounds? Who is controlling who should be collecting food and who should be working on housekeeping? Surely some queen ant is giving orders from a central communications hub, doing the geometry and topology and ensuring there are enough workers on each task? Biologists worked for years looking for this queen ant, completely sure that there had to be some centralized control, but to their great surprise, they never found one. There was no command structure, no hierarchy, no elite corps, no serf workers, no apparent organization at all. Yet although the colony appeared on first impressions to be totally anarchic, it was unmistakably an efficient, orderly, and highly successful society. It became clear to scientists that an ant colony, like many other structures in nature, was an example of a "self-organizing system"—a community that managed itself from the bottom up, not needing top-down chains of command in order to function.

In a time when abuses of power have put the church onto the front pages for all the wrong reasons, I believe it is vital that we learn something from these complex systems of organization that do not require power-hungry hierarchies. The key question is: how can high levels of organization be achieved without centralized control and structures of authority?

For the ants, the answer lies in the very seething mass of ants climbing over one another—the scrummage that appears to us as total anarchy but is actually for them the essential act of community. Ants are able to secrete different types of pheromone according to the activity they are engaged in. If they are collecting food, they leave a short pheromone trail communicating that, which other ants are able to read as they scramble over each other and around the colony. Ants have the ability not only to identify the different pheromone trails according to the different tasks but the gradient of the trail—whether it is getting stronger or weaker in a particular direction. Hence an ant might pick up a very strong trail that said, "There's loads of food over here," and by considering the strength and gradient of that trail, they could decide whether enough ants were already on that job (in which case they might instead go take out some trash) or whether some more help was needed.

What allows ants to self-organize, and what we need to learn from them, is this principle of low-level interaction and feedback. The colony works only because of the high number of interactions between ants. A stationary ant could not make an informed decision about which task to undertake because it would be out of the information loop, just as a "super ant" moving at ten times the speed of any other would be unable to lay trails, as well as leave them. Without the low-level, walking-pace interactions, the community could not self-organize, could not emerge.[2] Quite simply: no low-level feedback, no community.

Picking up the second example of a complex organism, Johnson then argues that our brains are organized along the same lines as ant colonies. Like them, there is no central command hub, no "super-cell" telling the others what to do. What links brains with ant colonies is the high level of networked interaction: just as with the ants, individual cells are in constant, simple communication with each other, feeding back information in the same way that ants read their trails, so that true impulses are reinforced and false ones are stamped out. Stretch. Breathe in. Look out. Scratch. Red light. Move right foot. Produce saliva. Listen. See. Think. Smell. Touch. Smile. Remember. On the microscopic, synaptic level it looks like anarchy—electrical impulses flying around with no apparent pattern and with no discernible sense—but look higher up at the colony or whole-brain level, and suddenly what seemed like chaos has a beautiful order and purpose to it. It is a huge self-organizing system, emergent and complex, intelligent and conscious . . . just like a buzzing and thriving city.

It was the striking similarities between some drawings of the brain and a city plan of historic Hamburg that had set Steven Johnson on his quest to discover just how similar their structures were—and he found that much like the brain, the ant colony, and so many other natural, complex systems, the cities we live in are organized on bottom-up rather than top-down principles. No central body legislates for the number of plumbers a city needs, but we are rarely left for days with broken pipes. There is no central system for ensuring enough food is imported into the city each day, but we don't periodically starve. This is because of the individuals on the ground reacting and responding to one another—seeing opportunities and gaps in the market, seizing new technological advances and putting them to use—all of these people and transactions interconnected through a dense web of *horizontal* connections, not needing to route everything up through to some queen ant controller or mayor before being given permission to act. As Jane Jacobs reflects, "No matter what you try to do to it, a city . . . *behaves* like a problem in organized complexity."[3]

Of course, like all natural systems, the places we live have had to evolve and develop over many, many years and, as Darwin would have predicted, some have done so more successfully than others: some ballooning in size and others diminishing as they responded to the environments they were in and the forces brought to bear on them. Like a brain, in their adolescence they were more susceptible to catastrophe as they did not have the experience, maturity, or corporate wisdom to deal effectively with their environment, as in the Great Chicago Fire or the 1929 Stock Market Crash. And like some of our brains, some of our communities have suffered dementia, schizophrenia, and dyslexia. They have lost their minds in intolerance and injustice, and sought to shake off foreign bodies in riots and lynchings. But these lapses in reason are testament to misunderstanding and inequality, to feedback systems breaking down and individuals not being prepared to listen, to other individuals not being prepared to take part in the system. Still others fly in endless circles at high speed, rendering themselves unable to assess the situation on the ground.

So although successful communities are not controlled by dictators, they do have to be regulated, bringing them above the genetic cut and thrust of "only the strong survive" to protect the vulnerable and weak, and ensure that sufficient controls are in place to enable society to function.[4] Traffic gets out of control in London, and a congestion charge is introduced—a modest regulation to adjust the flow conditions. High-tech express passes are offered for toll roads in the States. Planning regulations prevent houses from being built on parks and ensure that certain percentages of all new homes are designated "affordable." Incentives are put in place for developers to redevelop areas where industry has wilted so that different economic activity can move in where the old has left.

Communities have always had to evolve and adapt. From the mid-nineteenth century, society has grown into and beyond industrial, mechanistic places where workers had no say and were clocked in and out of linear production lines in rigid shifts, toward networked, devolved environ-

79

ments with flexible hours and teams working on multiple levels. Even at street level there have been architectural changes, which have promoted a networked, rather than individualistic, feel. In his book *Flesh and Stone*, which plots the history of the human body's relationship to the built environment, Richard Sennett writes:

> The planning of nineteenth century cities aimed to create a crowd of freely moving individuals, and to discourage the movement of organised groups through the city. Individual bodies moving through urban space gradually became detached from the space in which they moved, and the people from the space contained. As space became devalued through motion, individuals gradually lost a sense of sharing a fate with others.[5]

But now with evolution of new public spaces such as the South Bank in London, or the docks area of Bristol, people in the twenty-first century are being encouraged to meet in public rather than simply to use public spaces to move from one private place to another. Spaces such as the Tate Modern's Turbine Hall or Trafalgar Square have become more flexible, allowing a variety of uses: sitting, walking, meeting, performance, installation. In the US, the coffeehouse explosion is changing again the way people meet and work. Bryant Park in Manhattan is now an "Internet park" where people can stroll digitally as well as physically, all in a relaxed environment. In all of these places we are liberated from the technologies of movement, like the car, and released as spaces for the individual to pause and linger. These spaces may still have a primary function, but have become less rigid—allowing people to be at ease and spend "useless" or function-free time there. As Jane Jacobs summarizes, successfully planned cities are those where the planners have gotten into the habit of

1. thinking about processes;
2. working inductively, reasoning from particulars to the general, rather than the reverse.⁶

In other words, they have a sense of the interdependence of things, the movement and flows of people, and are prepared to work from the "bottom up." Thus, there is planning (which one can see as a form of regulation), but the success comes where this balance between regulation and freedom is just right. If there is too much regulation, a city is starved of creativity, entrepreneurial spirit, and character. Stalin's Soviet Union exemplified a system that was too stagnant and rigid—his top-down, hardwired principles of Communism simply didn't allow its inhabitants to live and function as free people. On the other hand, without enough regulation, abuses of power set in, leaving the poor and vulnerable to suffer—and the anarchy that leapt up in parts of post-Soviet Kazakhstan or Georgia are clear reminders of that.

In fact all bottom-up, emergent systems are regulated in some way in order to protect themselves from anarchy. Returning to the concept of the brain as one such system, Aldous Huxley (quoting William Blake[7]) wrote in the *Doors of Perception* of our brains being only just ajar, regulating the myriad simultaneous sensations of sight, sound, smell, touch, and thought down to a manageable trickle. Many "heads" in the 1960s took his writings on board and attempted to throw their "doors" open permanently through the use of LSD. Tom Wolfe's book *The Electric Kool-Aid Acid Test* brilliantly plots the journey of Ken Kesey and his Merry Pranksters as they discovered and then tried to "graduate" beyond acid into an eternal state of "unregulated perception"[8] . . . in the final analysis showing how destructive such mental deregulation can be. But equally destructive is the opposite extreme: total sensory deprivation. Flotation tanks, where sensations of sound, weight, light, touch, and smell are all either shut off or strongly regulated, are used by people for short periods to get a break from the hustle and bustle of the city, but sensory deprivation for sustained periods is well known as a source of torture and can quickly lead to mental collapse. At either extreme of anarchy and rigidity, it seems we are driven out of our minds.

This is the extraordinarily consistent truth about our cities, our brains, our ecosystems, and, I am suggesting, our churches: somewhere between these two poles of anarchy and rigidity—a spectrum with death at each end—there exists a place where a system begins to live, to self-organize, to become more than the sum of its parts, to develop a character, a culture, a *soul*, if you will—as if some breath has entered it and commanded it to live. If the pheromone trails are too short or last too long, the ant colony will not survive. If our senses are too stunted or our minds too levered open, we will die. Yet at some mystical place in between these two states of death, life is catalyzed into action; it sparks and takes hold, the exact conditions existing for consciousness to break out.

Regardless of the discipline we look at, the same truth rings out: "life" springs up in the complex region between rigidity and disorder. As the scientists like to say, life actually thrives right at the *edge* of chaos. In economic terms, that life is at the "edge of chaos" means that rigidity and anarchy will bring recession. In sociological terms, it means that a healthy society can only develop where it is *nearly* chaotic, but not quite; free, yet stable. In spiritual terms, that life exists at the edge of chaos means that the conjunctive church will emerge only when it has located itself between rigid fundamentalism and anarchic liberty. Christ's incarnation was God's radical repositioning of himself right on that edge: a vulnerable child in a chaotic world. As we seek the church's reincarnation, we must seek to position ourselves in the same dangerous place of complex life.

And all these places of life *are* complex. In the world of mechanical systems it was possible to predict exactly what output could be expected from any given input. Things were seemingly rigidly connected by levers and rods, so that pressing Button A moved a fixed system of linkages that waved Hand B, and there was no way it could do anything else. This is how we understood economics, chemistry, biology, urban planning, and computing—and it still seems to be how we understand church.

Build these apartments and this will happen. Raise interest rates and that will happen. Put on this *Alpha* course and this will happen. By its rigid cause-and-effect linkages, the mechanistic world condemns us, allowing us no freedom or doubt, no room for error, no grace, no mercy.

Where the mechanical world condemned us, the complex world brings us life. Somewhere between the rigid mechanics that locks us into fixed places and the anarchy of unregulated freedom that refuses us any locus lies a mysterious, graceful place where we begin to live, to adapt, to put down roots, to evolve, to understand for ourselves and create.

There is an irresistible force of movement encompassing science, industry, architecture, and education, which is shifting everything from a modernist, mechanistic, deterministic, Newtonian, Laplacian worldview toward this complex, networked, Einsteinian, evolving one. It would be foolish if the church was left behind, for it seems the whole of civilization is gradually catching up with what nature already knew, and God already undertook—the vital risk of rebirth, of re-emerging . . . of shedding the rigid, top-down, authoritarian, unadaptable, prehistoric ways that rendered the dinosaurs unable to meet the challenge of their changed environment and ultimately left them as fossils, the pressures of stone crushing them.

The Empty Church

They laid this stone trap
for him, enticing him with candles,
as though he would come like some huge moth
out of the darkness to beat there.
Ah, he had burned himself
before in the human flame
and escaped, leaving the reason
torn. He will not come any more
to our lure. Why, then, do I kneel still
striking my prayers on a stone
heart? Is it in hope one
of them will ignite yet and throw
on its illumined walls the shadow
of someone greater than I can understand?

R. S. Thomas[9]

God will not come anymore, will no longer be lured into our stone traps. And yet against this huge force of evolutionary movement, the bulk of the church stands rigidly still under precarious arrangements of stones. If we cannot adapt, the pressures of them will crush us too and form our fossilized homes, leaving us to museums and history books.

Living in emerging, complex, bottom-up communities, we attend churches that are hugely top-down, mechanistic, obsessed with hierarchy and authority. Often wrapped in the guise of "accountability," our leaders enforce dictatorial structures ensuring that every sign of life is routed through them, that nothing is given the go-ahead without their blessing—and this need for blessing from on high usually acts as the curse of death on innovative, creative, and cutting-edge ideas. Inspired fledglings have their wings clipped as they are forced to justify their ideas and come up with completely "sorted" plans that fit in with a monochrome vision.

We should not ask this of our children. The newly emerged, the newborn, must be allowed to make mistakes, to risk, to dribble and scribble. In a church that admits it is "not holding, winning or discipling young people," there needs to be a radical reassessment of how we treat our young, a move to "release and support young people who are leaders among their peers."[10] Christ could not begin his ministry immediately after he was born, and neither should we expect every sprouting of new growth to be fully formed and fully able to defend itself. So much of the church still demands immediate results from every new initiative and idea—still demands revolution.

"Listen," God says, "I am doing a new thing. Do you not perceive it?" Complexity theory warns us we *must* listen because old-order top-down systems cannot survive in an emerging, evolving world. There will be no more revolution, only evolution. As the *New York Times* proclaimed, this "isn't just a fascinating quirk of science; it's the future."[11]

Yet if science warns us that a rigid, top-down church will not survive in an emergent world, it is also clear that a totally deregulated, anarchic church will do no better. Without any checks or balances, it will disperse into obscurity, having no mechanisms for feedback and therefore no way of learning and evolving. So if the church is to survive in the modern urban environment, it must learn to find new peaks out of the valleys by re-emerging as a complex, self-organizing system. It must be born again at the edge of chaos, just as the rigid, Old Testament God was. It must become embryonic and re-evolve within a host culture, learning from it, feeding from it, and growing to understand it from the inside out. We must reestablish ourselves as the *body* of Christ, not the machine of Christ. Bodies are organic, dynamic, sentient, and conscious. They have hearts. Machines break down, while bodies evolve. This metaphorical re-centering from machine to body will require us to rethink our language too, away from the industrial vocabulary of "structure," "drive," "mechanism," "steering" toward more body-centered language: "nourish," "grow," "nurture," "cultivate," and "adapt."

There are still those who cry for revolution, for a revival that will change things in a snap, make everything OK as thousands flock to church . . . But the days of revolution are over. The cry for revival is too often a cry of abdication: *you* do it all, God. Well, God has done God's bit—it is the systems that now need to change. This is the faith we have signed up for: the church as the body of Christ where we have real parts to play, real responsibilities.

We must not act rashly—diving in to this or that. We must do as God did. Stop. Wait. Grieve. Strip away power, might, pretense at knowledge, riches . . . and be born again. As Einstein famously said, "The same consciousness that created a problem cannot solve it." We need genuine newness. Just as a butterfly is not "more caterpillar," we need to re-emerge as a totally new organism, one that is adapted to the complex and evolving environment of the unique, local places we inhabit; one operating with a spirituality that rejects simplistic, monochrome, flat answers and embraces the multidimensional, full-color complexity of our situation, as R. S. Thomas so beautifully describes:

Emerging

Not as in the old days I pray,
God. My life is not what it was.
Yours, too, accepts the presence of
the machine? Once I would have asked
healing. I go now to be doctored,
to drink sinlessly of the blood
of my brother, to lend my flesh
as manuscript of the great poem

of the scalpel. I would have knelt
long, wrestling with you, wearing
you down. Hear my prayer, Lord, hear
my prayer. As though you were deaf, myriads
of mortals have kept up their shrill
cry, explaining your silence by
their unfitness.
             It begins to appear
this is not what prayer is about.
It is the annihilation of difference,
the consciousness of myself in you,
of you in me; the emerging
from the adolescence of nature
into the adult geometry
of the mind. I begin to recognise
you anew, God of form and number.
There are questions we are the solution
to, others whose echoes we must expand
to contain. Circular as our way
is, it leads not back to that snake-haunted
garden, but onward to the tall city
of glass that is the laboratory of the spirit.

                              R. S. Thomas[12]

The Character of the
Emergent Church

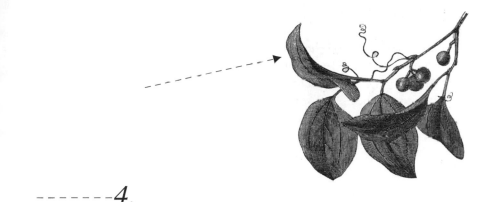

-------4.

{ The Character of the Emergent Church }

Before returning to the Christ narrative and exploring how the principles of emergence affected his ministry and passion, I want to take an extended aside and look in some detail at what complexity might mean for the church in more practical terms. That there is perhaps more scientific thinking presented here than many are used to, I make no excuses for. In the spirit of balance that this book is advocating, I believe poets and scientists need to explore their interdependence and not be polarized into mutual suspicion; I hope both will find some gift here.

If life exists at the edge of chaos, it exists there in a state that denies us the power to predict where it might spring next and what form it might take. Who at the dawn of creation would have foreseen elephants and fireflies, zebras and monkey puzzle trees? So in praying for the church to evolve, for it to become a conjunctive, self-organizing, bottom-up system that can incarnate and adapt to our local situations, we must resist the temptation to arrest its development by saying what it is going to look like before we really have any idea.

Talk of the "emerging church" is rife. A recent seminar around the subject at the annual Greenbelt arts festival in the UK gave rise to mention of pub nights for bikers, various uses of Mongolian tents, "café church," meetings for young moms, and mixing Taizé with "Ancient and Modern" as signs of this "emerging." Almost without exception these things are explained in terms of attempts to "be postmodern" and "engage with the culture." I am sure that they are all valid signs of change, and should be encouraged as "signs of life," but do they point to genuine *emergence*? We need to distinguish carefully between talk of "emerging church" and the "Emergent Church." I am sure that some of the activities cited as evidence of the emerging church in that seminar, and in the stories contained in reports such as *Mission-Shaped Church*,[1] will be part of the future Emergent Church, but we need to be aware that while these things may well display genuine newness, they are currently small pockets of fresh practice existing in a non-emergent whole.[2] My problem with many of these emerging church projects is that they are still attempting to bring church up-to-date by "trainspotting" some aspect of culture and making church fit it. I want to argue that in the Emergent Church the emphasis will be on being the train, rather than trainspotting: rather than trying to import culture into church and make it "cool," we need instead to become "wombs of the divine" and completely rebirth the church into a host culture. So while the excitement over the emerging church is to be welcomed, I think we need to advance with caution for fear of these things precipitating a revolution that will not last, and bringing changes that will be just tactical.

One of the areas that is perhaps most talked about as evidence of the emerging church is the "alternative worship" scene. Certainly, with most such groups having formed from the bottom up rather than as part of an established church leader's vision, there are elements of emergence in them. However, like many of these activities hailed as part of the emerging church, alternative worship groups are rarely conjunctive organizations, and it seems more likely to me from my inside view that alternative worship will be seen in the future to have been part of the preparation of the ground for the new to emerge from, rather than the newness itself.

Perhaps the best comparison that can be made is to punk in the late 1970s. Punk was never going to be the future of music. Its savage energy was unsustainable and as a movement it was always destined to sell out, to assimilate, to self-destruct. Many commentators now look back and see "pure" punk really existing for only about eight months in 1976–77. Yet its effect on the cultural landscape has been enormous. It is not just the huge *number* of bands, artists, and other creatives who refer to punk as an influence that is staggering, but the massively wide *scope* of those that do too. Bands from U2 to the Smiths to Happy Mondays to the Prodigy to Massive Attack to Beastie Boys, to graphic artists from Peter Saville to The Designers Republic have all expressed punk as part of their inspiration. How could a music so essentially raw and fierce spawn all of this? The answer seems to be that punk gave people permission. It drove through and trashed the ivory towers of the music business, dismantling all the perceived wisdom about musicianship, marketing, profit, contracts, and boundaries. Punk razed culture to the ground. It burnt like a bushfire and exposed the full horizon of the possibilities of music and art to a generation who were then empowered to pick up whatever instruments and tools they had, and create. As Johnny Rotten said in an interview for *Sounds* in 1976: "I hate hippies and what they stand for. I hate long hair. I hate pub bands. . . . I want people to see us and start something, or else I'm just wasting my time." Start *something*. Anything. Nobody before had told them they could, nobody before had told them it didn't matter what it sounded or looked like anyway.

Later that year, on June 4, the Sex Pistols played Manchester Lesser Free Trade Hall. Among the tiny crowd of one hundred or so were people who would turn out to be some of the most important names behind music in the UK for the next twenty years, including Peter Hook and Bernard Sumner (who went on to form Joy Division and New Order), Morrissey, Tony Wilson (who formed Factory Records to support the new music scene in Manchester that blossomed as a result of the gig—and gave us A Certain Ratio, the Haçienda club, "Madchester," and the rave scene of the late 1980s), Howard Devoto and Pete Shelley (who were inspired that night to form the Buzzcocks), and Mick Hucknall.

This gig is seen as punk's climax. Within eighteen months the Sex Pistols had imploded and punk—"the great rock-and-roll swindle"—had gone up in smoke. "Wake up," as Will Self said. "The avant-garde is dead—it's been marketed."[3] Yet punk had done its work. It had had a hugely cathartic effect on the music industry, and by tearing down these structures the way had been cleared for major new directions to be explored by those who came after it. None of this could have been predicted by the music the Sex Pistols were playing themselves. There is no hint of "Blue Monday" in "Pretty Vacant."

In the same way, although the alternative worship scene and other fresh expressions may be producing innovative ways of being church, I believe their primary function will be simply to clear the ground and give permission to the wider church to imagine new things. Just as punk was never going to be the future of music, so alternative worship cannot be the future of the church. It may help people to weather the storms of Stage 4, but it is not the Conjunctive Church that we seek. Like punk, it too requires energy that is unsustainable, and it too is beginning to be diluted into the mainstream without having actually transformed it. It too suffers from mythic numbers with many claiming to be involved, but few actually making it.

The *Mission-Shaped Church* report appears to express concern over alternative worship groups' longevity, stating that "it is a cause of major celebration when an alt.worship community lasts ten years."[4] Yet punk's story encourages us to look beyond timescales and numbers. It will be interesting to see what becomes of those who are inspired by alternative worship, who are shown a faith without boundaries by it and given permission by it to pick up instruments and simply create. But what newness will come out of this we cannot yet say.

There may not be any clues to the shape of the Emergent Church in current alternative worship practice, even if in years to come people look back and say they were inspired by it.

Studies of self-organizing, emergent systems have shown similar traits running through them, whether they are in computing, biology, or economics. In every area of life it seems there are historically top-down organizations that are having to adapt and evolve; that have realized that the only way that they can survive is to transform themselves from Stage 3, monolithic, flabby, grey institutions that do not and cannot respond to realities on the ground, into conjunctive, devolved, bottom-up, adaptable networks that are trim, agile, and flexible enough to face and meet the ever-changing challenges of the fast-moving post-Enlightenment world.

So we are not alone. Indeed, as mentioned earlier, it is perhaps pertinent that the church is going to have to learn about its own survival from so-called secular institutions that are going to be treading the complex path with it. Remember again: Christ was not independent from his host culture—he needed it, he fed from it and was happy to learn from it, and we should be too. Our current situation will *require* us to stop and ask for help from those around us. We cannot take the all new and shiny Emergent Church off the shelf at some ecclesiastic superstore, no matter how wealthy we may be and how much we may be able to invest in new furniture configurations and AV equipment . . . It is unknown to us. It cannot be predicted or grown in a petri dish, it cannot be hybridized from already available parts. No genetic modification is going to speed its coming or increase its yield. We simply have to get the mix of constituent initial conditions right, and wait for the miracle of creation and evolution to take its course. A journey of risky freedom that God took with creation so long ago stands before us now. We have the power to create automatons, but we must have the love of freedom to allow genuine newness to evolve.

Welcome to the cloud of unknowing. Exciting, isn't it, to feel the spirit of adventure, of risk . . . an element of danger and tension? There is no stagnant air here, just the invigorating funk of new life in the making, of new ground being broken and moldy trestle tables being turned over in the temples, church halls, and moneylenders' offices. . . .

Welcome back to the birthplace of punk, to London's King's Road in June 1976, to a reverent iconoclasm, a clearing of the decks and jack-hammering of foundations, to tilling of soil and preparation of new ground . . . to the sweating, heart-recovering quiet as we stop and wait for what we have set to grow and live. And there are no ecclesiastic Rolf Harrises who can tell what it is yet—indeed we should be cautious of those who claim to be able to tell. As Christ warned: "The kingdom of God does not come with your careful observation, nor will people be able to say, 'Here it is,' or 'There it is'" (Luke 17:20–21). It is not to be pointed at or visited and studied and taken back and replicated. Workshops will not be able to mow it down with bullet points, and training manuals will not be able to ensure its success in your area. Why not? "Because," as Christ continued, "the kingdom of God is within you and among you." It is the mustard seed, the yeast that works its way unseen through the dough.

If churches are going to be reborn, to emerge and evolve as self-organizing systems, then they are going to do so as organisms adapted to their unique environment. Why do leopards have spots and tigers stripes? Only local knowledge can help answer that question. The success or otherwise of "the kingdom" in our area is "within us." The answers lie "among us" in our shared, networked, distributed knowledge of the particular space we inhabit, whether geographical, social, or cultural. The key cannot be found from without in some general formula for success, just as Danny Hillis's number-sorting program could not be written from the top down. It must be conceived, nurtured, birthed, and given space to evolve from within.

Characteristics of Emergent Systems

Emergent systems are open systems

Although we cannot possibly predict what *shape* the Emergent Church will have, we can describe some of the *characteristics* it is likely to display. We cannot know its full-grown features, but we can examine its genes. Our first observation is that systems that are likely to evolve are characterized by being *open* as opposed to *closed*. A good example of an organic open system can probably be found very close by. If you are out walking in the park or woods, then it is very likely that some slime mold (*Dictyostelium discoideum*) will be lurking nearby in some damp, cool place. If you did come across it, it would appear to be a grim-looking ochre slime that was totally stationary, but return to the same spot a few days later and you would find it might have moved on or even disappeared, apparently into thin air. This strange nomadic/Houdini existence of slime mold fascinated scientists, who through research discovered that it actually exists in and constantly switches between two distinct states.[5] For much of the time, when food supplies and conditions are good, slime mold cells exist as distinct units, totally independent from other cells nearby. But when food gets short and the environment more challenging, the individual cells coalesce and act as a single organism, which begins to crawl quietly across the ground, munching wood and other rotting organic material until it finds better conditions, whereupon the cells disband and seem to disappear.

What is important for our purposes is to understand that this change-from-within is triggered *by* the environment in which the slime mold is existing, and that central to its survival is its ability to read and respond to this environment. If the slime mold was unable to do this—was a system closed off from its environment—it would quickly die, just as any church sealed off from the outside world will die too.

The educationalist Keith Morrison, reflecting on the place complexity theory has in school leadership, notes that "for a system to survive it cannot rely on introspection and closure, it must be open to the environment; sensing it, responding to it and, in turn, shaping it."[6] The slime mold system is constantly engaging with its environment and is being changed by it, just as the environment another complex system—is constantly engaging with the slime mold and being changed by it too.[7]

In a closed system this sort of outside influence is discouraged and seen as "infection." In an open system, it is positively encouraged and seen as "cross-fertilization." As John Donne put it, "No man is an island, entire of itself."[8] We do not exist as closed systems ourselves: we have to ingest matter to sustain us, we have to relate to others outside of us if we are to exist as healthy people. Indeed, if we did try to become entirely closed systems, we would very quickly die.

It is interesting to note that those who have attempted to become virtually "biologically closed" systems by fasting have always in turn seen their social or spiritual sides become more open, as if to compensate. Whether the illusionist David Blaine actually did fast for forty-four days in the autumn of 2003 is a moot point—the fact is that, illusion or real, it seems that he felt he had to do so suspended from a crane in a transparent case for everyone to see. Whether he could have lasted that long without the constant interaction from the crowds who gathered is another matter. As a parallel example, Christ's fast in the desert was in no way a "closing off" of himself from his environment but rather a radical exercise in opening and sensitizing himself to it as he began his ministry to engage fully with it. So in both cases—the illusionist who has almost divine pretensions and the divinity tempted to perform illusions—what might appear as a model promoting the benefits of being a closed system attempting perfect equilibrium with itself in actual fact turns out to espouse the essentiality of disequilibrium for personal development.

Thinking about the "retreat" culture that exists in many parts of modern Christianity, one has to conclude that attempts to see retreats as "closing off" and "trying to find equilibrium" are going to prove ultimately unsatisfying. Perhaps then when we do voluntarily minimize interaction in one area of our existence—through solitude, fasting, etc.—we should not use these times for introspection and closure but for maximizing our openness in other areas. For just as stagnant water cannot support life, so closed systems in equilibrium are bound to die.

As Morrison says, "Systems *need* disequilibrium to survive."[9] Applying this to the organism that is the church, we can be sure that the Emergent Church that we seek will be characterized by a sense of being open to its environment, of "sensing it, responding to it and, in turn, shaping it." This as opposed to the prevailing current mode of closure characterized by self-sufficiency.

Looking at the microscopic level, the boundary between the slime mold and its environment is actually very blurred—it is not easy to distinguish which is which—and in the same way, in the Emergent, open-system Church we would expect to see a very blurred boundary between local community activity and specifically church activity. For many this will be seen as "dirty"[10]—as infecting the good and pure activities of the church—but it is precisely this blurred boundary, with no hard line between in and out, that will be allowing the church to sense, respond to, and shape the community. For others, this blurring will be experienced as rocking the boat—upsetting their equilibrium and their comfortable place with "no alarms and no surprises." Too many people currently scatter themselves on pews for a sense of comfort and tradition—an escape from the outside—and to suggest that the outside should be brought in will be very threatening. But the closed-system churches with aging and unchanging congregations are literally dying and wilting, entombed in buildings with massive potential to resource local community life—yet which are clad with citadel doors and iron locks.

If the Emergent Church is going to be an open system, then it will have to be a place of blurred boundaries rather than fixed lines, and of disequilibrium rather than homeostasis, in order to respond to and engage with its environment.

Emergent systems are adaptable systems

It is also significant to note that the environment to which the slime mold is responding is highly localized, and that for all emergent systems the nature of self-organization is dictated by local, not global, circumstances. Hence an Emergent Church as an open system may have an entirely different shape and structure from another church only a mile or two away, and successful practice in one system may not translate at all to the other. What will be key for both is that by being open to their environment and seeking to respond to it they are being open to *adapting* to its unique and localized needs.

It is tempting in our society of standardized computer ports, off-the-shelf everything, and prepackaged solutions, to look for ready-made models of church or worship that we can buy into. It seems to work in Iona, so let's do Celtic. The *Alpha* course seems to work in Kensington, so let's translate it into Swahili. They seem to be doing well in Willow Creek, let's give it a go in Burnt Oak. While cross-fertilization of ideas is to be encouraged, unless they are adapted to the local situation, they run the risk of failing to thrive.

As previously mentioned, the church is not an independent, closed organism that has all the resources it needs for its own indefinite survival. We are hosted by a culture, and in order to survive in that culture (which has shown over the past fifty years that it can survive pretty well without us), we must open ourselves to it and adapt to it. We can have absolutely no chance of shaping it unless we can sense and respond to it, and this means adapting our interfaces, our "ports" if you will, to allow free transfer each way. Of course, there are those who still see the church as a holy lifeboat, attempting to save as many as possible from the sinking vessel that is modern culture, and that any attempt to adapt to it will result in us getting pulled down too, but it seems impossible to defend this position when we read of a God who got stuck in and involved in a culture at every conceivable level. Indeed, Christ was very careful to align his practice so that people could engage with him with the greatest of ease. He spoke in stories using their vernacular and idiom, lived in and out of their homes, and depended on them for food and resources at every turn. He was in the proper sense a "beggar"—a word that comes to us from the *Beghards*, a community of wandering friars who, like other mendicants of the day, relied wholly on gifts to survive. We need to imitate Christ and return to a radical reliance on our local communities for survival; culturally and socially we need to be dependent on them, not independent of them.[11]

Emergent systems are learning systems

If a system is open and attempting to adapt to its environment, it must always be seeking to learn: to sense what is going on around it and process this information intelligently to make changes. This virtuous cycle of sensing, learning, adapting, and changing has led some writers on complexity to state their belief that change *equals* learning: that *any* exposure to a different situation can help us learn *something* positive and help us to adapt better to our environment. It is perhaps easier to see the truth of this by looking at the opposite end of the spectrum: a mind that is static, that is sealed from any outside influence, cannot learn anything new.

Reflecting on my own background in education, it is ironic that many schools—as centers of learning—are actually very poor at learning and responding to their environment themselves. In education we tend to talk of schools showing emergent properties not so much as "self-organizing" as "self-renewing," and the schools that do display these properties view learning as a culture that permeates the whole system. Many researchers are now seeing that, rather than helping a system toward renewal, Ofsted, the national school inspection body in the UK, can present itself as so threatening to schools that very little learning actually takes place: the system goes into paralyzing shock and finds itself unable to take on board some of the good advice that might be present beneath the huge pile of intense scrutiny. The problem that Ofsted and other large inspection bodies suffer from is that they are tending to make schools approach the problem of change from the angle of revolution, rather than the evolutionary approach that is more likely to bring about transformation. The revolutions that schools attempt in the face of Ofsted tend to produce tactical changes, which leave the body of the organization feeling cynical and disenfranchised, and research shows that post-Ofsted, schools tend to go into a slump as staff recover, which has a measurable negative effect on performance.

Many of our churches actually seem to lie at completely the opposite end of the scale from this form of inspection (not that I am suggesting an ecclesiastic inspection system, amusing as a *Monty Python* sketch based on it might be). By this I mean there seems to be a total lack of analysis of what is actually going on. If an analysis is to be done, it is important that it must also be of the right kind. As Manuel de Landa warns, "Analyzing a whole into parts and then attempting to model it by *adding up* the components will fail to capture the property that emerged from complex interactions."[12]

In other words, vertical analysis cannot detect horizontal, networked connections. De Landa uses the rain forest as a good example: it is fine to study it top-down, starting with the forest and dividing it into species, but this will tell us nothing about the interdependence of animals and plants and therefore nothing about how the whole ecosystem works. Relating this to how churches ought to be sensing, learning, and adapting, there needs to be horizontal analysis of how the different parts are interrelating, how the ecosystem of the church is functioning, in order for us to be able to feed it and sustain it. It is worth being reminded again about Jane Jacobs's words that a successfully planned city is one that is planned with a view to process, and a view to working "inductively, reasoning from the particulars to the general, rather than the reverse."[13] In such a city, the interrelatedness is taken into account by those leading it, and this is what gives it a sense of life. Again, we find that for an organization to live—to grow and evolve and adapt and renew—it must position itself somewhere in between the two poles of heavy-handed inspection and complete nonreflection.

In all emergent systems we see that the cycle of sensing, learning, adapting, and changing is one that is going on constantly. It is not parachuted in every four years for a big shake-up but permeates the whole organism and is continually effecting changes quietly in the background. Many who have written about the application of this form of change to organizations have referred to Japanese industry's tradition of *Kaizen*, which emphasizes a process of continuous small-scale improvement. There are no grand meetings where the board members decree how the company is going to change. Rather, each member of the company and each team within it is encouraged to continually reflect on any small ways in which they could improve their work or workplace—and the cumulative effect of these tiny incremental changes over time is large-scale transformation. Through *Kaizen* the company is constantly responding and adapting. Again, this is a mode of operation that carries some risks and requires a real culture of trust because the board is not actually going to be in total control. It is not going to be prescribing exactly how people do their jobs, but will give people goals and a framework within which to achieve them in the best way they can.

The Emergent Church will be a place where the *Kaizen* principle is in effect. It will be an open place, fully engaging with the environment that is hosting it; sensing it, responding to it, learning from it, always seeking to change and evolve and renew itself. In his book *The Intelligence Advantage: Organizing for Complexity*, Michael McMaster suggests that an organization that is learning in this way will have:

- an ability within its structures to receive, understand, and interpret, in various ways, signals from the external environment;
- an ability to respond in various ways to those signals, including creating new internal structures and organizational features; and
- an ability to influence the external environment both proactively and reactively.[14]

He then goes on to state that "the rate at which [an organization] learns determines its ability to adapt, innovate and ultimately survive in a changing . . . environment."[15] So if the church is going to adapt and survive, to learn in this way or at least increase our rate of learning, we are going to have to become far more strategic and explore structures that can "receive, understand and interpret . . . signals from the external environment." This sort of language brings us back to the example of our brains as emergent, complex systems, and it is precisely in this kind of *Kaizen* way that our brains themselves learn. The only reason they can do this is because of their highly networked structure, and this allows our brains to engage in the fundamental activity required for networked learning: feedback.

To take a simple example of just how superior a system that integrates feedback is over one that doesn't, imagine two robots programmed to run a hot bath for you. Most baths in the UK have two separate faucets for hot and cold water, run from central tanks in the house, meaning that pressures can easily change when water is used elsewhere in the house. In such a system the non-feedback robot might be able to measure the temperature and volume of the water in your hot-water tank, even the temperature of the air in the bathroom and of the bath itself. It would then use a preprogrammed calculation to work out how much hot and cold water to add and how long to run the faucets for. It would turn them on, leave the room to do some other robot duties, and then come back exactly on time to turn the faucets off. Which would be all well and good, so long as nothing changed once the faucets had been turned on. But if someone came in and flushed the toilet, or washed their hands, or opened the window, the conditions that the calculations were based on would change, and your bath would be the wrong temperature. Not only that, but the non-feedback robot would have no ability to sense that these changes had happened and do anything about it.

For the robot with feedback integrated, the changing conditions do not present any problem. Having made the calculations, it then sticks around and takes regular measurements of the temperature. Not only that—for knowledge that things are going wrong is no help when you are powerless to change them—but this feedback of information informs its decision to make fine adjustments to the taps, so you get a perfect bath every time.[16]

This feedback robot, while great, does still lack one essential characteristic: learning. In its current form, no matter how many times you opened the window or flushed the toilet, it still would not remember what it had to do last time this happened to get the temperature right. In this way, it is being purely reactive, not proactive. For the robot to learn, to truly show some sign of life or intelligence, it would have to have some kind of memory and consciously be able to make adjustments *before* things went wrong. It is this powerful combination of feedback and memory that makes our brains such effective learners.

The memory aspect is fundamental for any form of advanced evolution, because the brain doesn't want to use precious sensing power on previously learned basics, such as walking. Reflecting back on Brueggemann's notion that "only memory allows possibility," we can now see that without memory we are left without the possibility of evolving or learning. Like the amnesiac feedback robot, we can still survive—reacting and responding to each new situation and getting by—but we cannot bring any experience to these situations and have to relearn them all over again each time.

One might then reflect that perhaps we are living in a society that is gradually losing its memory. As culture accelerates we live increasingly in the present moment, unwilling to take the time to bring the wisdom and past experiences of other generations or backgrounds to bear on the situations we face. So we go to war, just as our predecessors went to war. We vote in right-wing extremists, just as they did. We point at new Christian leaders and say this is it, this is the future. We vote each new pop star the greatest of all time, and each newly acclaimed film the best of the new century . . . We do this because we are losing the essential connectivity that allows distributed, communal knowledge and experience to be shared. With our eyes suckling from cathode-ray nipples feeding us a skimmed diet of soap opera and home improvements, we have lost the ability and mental space to simply talk and share thoughts and receive wisdom. We are in "future shock"—the pace of change is so great that our human, evolutionary systems simply cannot cope. Part of the prophetic role of the Emergent Church will be to encourage society to recover its memory and have a healthy balance between past, present, and future:

> Christ has died,
> Christ is risen,
> Christ will come again.

The Emergent Church must be allowed to learn in the same way as we do: by making connections, trying new things, and always sensing, getting feedback, adapting, and remembering. The feedback that is central to this sort of learning is not a hardwired or particularly conscious process. Thinking back to the self-organizing ant colony, the feedback that allows them to communicate what task they are involved in is extremely simple. If it were any more complicated than sensing the basic pheromone trails, then it would take too much time and the colony would grind to a halt in analysis.

Applying this to the Emergent Church, we can expect it to be characterized by connectivity and simple systems of feedback as it seeks to be a learning, self-renewing organization. It will be committed to sensing changes in its environment and through this be able to adapt and respond to them, as well as use its memory and wisdom to preempt change and actually influence its environment too. This is an impossible task for a single leader or a strongly hierarchical leadership structure. A commitment to being adaptable and open to the environment will require a commitment to distributed leadership.

Emergent systems have distributed knowledge

Thinking again about the brain, let us not forget that there is no one super-cell storing all of this information about shared experience and learned connections. Because this knowledge-store is distributed, constituent cells can be continually replaced without any perceivable loss of brain function. Perhaps the clearest example of another distributed knowledge system is the Internet. The concept of a dispersed network of computers was specifically designed by the US military to enable them to withstand a nuclear holocaust: even if a number of individual computers were taken out by the blast, the military network could still function normally because the "knowledge" —or data—was distributed across hundreds of different "cells" in different parts of the country.

This having blossomed into the World Wide Web, we now have a system so distributed with so many millions of individual terminals involved that only a large-scale destruction of the developed world could begin to take it down.

In stark contrast, top-down systems are characterized by very centralized knowledge—and hence very centralized power. The early church Gnostics with their "secret knowledge" were not the first (and won't be the last) to realize the power of holding knowledge back and sharing it only with a select few. More recently politicians seem to have reveled in the power they have over people, with intelligence being massaged behind the scenes, and their issues of general threat alerts about terror attacks from unnamed groups—all based on information they are not at liberty to reveal to us. Knowledge is power—and the powerful know that, so use their power to restrict the distribution of it and thereby remain powerful.[17]

The Emergent Church—like all emergent systems—will not be marked by knowledge stored centrally. There will be no key leader who will be seen as the fount of all knowledge and wisdom on all topics. The distributed nature of knowledge will be positively celebrated, as it will prevent the collecting of power into small male-dominated pools, and thus protect people from the abuses that that power would bring. In turn, narrow preaching of Scripture will be avoided and understanding of it will become a shared project.

This in turn will mean that the idea of truth in the Emergent Church will change. It will no longer reside in some intangible conceptual work of theology that only the fully trained and ordained can unlock. Instead, the pursuit of it will be about our shared experience. Some will bring their wisdom from the church's history, others a story from their social work, still others a passage from Scripture, and others a song or poem. Such organizations beyond Stage 3 or Stage 4 are not just about wishy-washy relativism but have "a radical openness to the truth [that] stems from their confidence in the reality mediated by its own tradition and in the awareness that that reality overspills their mediation."[18] It is about an open dedication to understanding that each of us has a contribution to make, that no one is worthless, that no one person can have the final say on what is true. Of course, over time, the connections and associations that are positively reinforced over and over will become established in the memory and collective consciousness—but this will not be due to one person's input and not stored in one person's mind. There will no longer be a single external authority to which people look for truth, but rather a distributed network of authorities that people look to in order to assimilate multiple perspectives on truth.

This conceptual battle, between a single external authority holding the truth and a distributed network of knowledge, is one that has been raging in the software industry for many years. The computer giant Microsoft is a proponent of the "closed truth" model: their code for their software is a very closely guarded secret that only the privileged few get access to. The disadvantages of this approach have been exposed recently with security flaws discovered by hackers and exploited with viruses. Because the code is such a closely guarded secret, the flaws have to be corrected by a small team of people, and thus the "antidote" can take many months to be found. Other software systems, such as Linux, take an "open source" approach. Their code is freely available for anyone to look at, and thus a huge network of people is constantly tinkering and updating it, constantly sending in ideas and improvements. Similar security issues and bugs are therefore fixed very quickly as so many people are able to bring their expertise to the problem. Not only that, but the system becomes far more adaptable and flexible, as people can modify the code to suit their own local needs. This is the "radical openness to the truth" that Fowler is talking about. The truth of the church needs to become "open source," with distributed agents able to feed in solutions, rather than it being left to a closed clique of experts.

This concept of distributed agents providing positive reinforcement is also central to emerging systems. Returning to the idea of feedback, we see that there are actually two sorts: negative and positive. Negative feedback regulates a system, rather like the robot regulating the flow of hot water. It tends to intervene and pull systems back when they are in danger of deviating too far from the perceived norm.

111

All organizations need people who perform this role—and they must be given adequate voice to be useful.

Positive feedback does not so much use information gathered to regulate but to actually feed and encourage more growth. Those of you who have used eBay or Amazon's online secondhand book service will be aware of the star-rating system given to buyers and sellers. If you are intending to buy something from someone on the site, you can look at how many "stars" they have and how many feedback comments from previous transactions this is based on. Thus a seller with five stars from two hundred transactions has a proven track record in reliability and so is more likely to attract even more sales. The positive feedback is actually accelerating growth, not restricting it.

An example perhaps more pertinent to the question of distributed knowledge and truth in the church is that of Slashdot—a web-based discussion forum.[19] In its early days it had very few problems with "spammers" (people posting useless junk messages) or "cranks" (people expressing completely ridiculous and spurious views). The volume of postings was small enough for Slashdot's creator, Rob Malda, to filter most of the junk out. As time went by, the volume of postings grew massively, and it became impossible for him to cope. In the end he came up with a system based on the positive feedback principles of emergent systems—and this is how Slashdot continues to survive as a serious forum today.

The idea is simple: all posts to the site are given a rating. Contributors therefore build up an average rating score based on the number and the quality of their previous contributions. Those who consistently write quality articles get consistently high ratings, and their posts are therefore given a higher priority on the site. This links well with Fowler's description of Stage 5 organizations or people as those being able to process truth not simply through the "self-certainty of the knower" but by the "trustworthiness of the known."[20]

The people doing the rating are chosen at random from the large pool of those who have used the site a number of times. When chosen as one of these "moderators," you are asked to rate contributions made by other users on a scale of –1 to +5. Each chosen moderator has only a finite number of "points" they can allocate, so after a certain number of ratings, their time as moderator is over; Malda compares it to doing jury service. The final aspect of the system is that the higher your average rating on the site, the more chance you have of being invited to become a moderator. In this way, through a completely bottom-up process, leaders and shared "truth" can rise naturally to the surface.

Two key points are pertinent here. First, if you go to the Slashdot site, you can choose to view it at your own "quality threshold." In other words, if you want the completely unregulated, anything-goes version with all posts expressing any views, you can have it. The system is not about eliminating dissenting voices or unpleasantness, it is about allowing quality to rise.[21] Second, if people are not prepared to take their responsibilities as moderators seriously, the system will quickly fall apart. It requires commitment, a corporate spirit, for it to work. In the same way, the distributed knowledge of the Internet works only if people are able to keep their terminals or servers switched on.

I imagine the Emergent Church taking such a model and making it work in a "real" community, rather than a "virtual" one. What exact form this will take should not be predicted at this stage, but the principle of distributed truth evolving through networks of trust is a powerful one that will allow the church to step away from the accusations of bigotry, arrogance, and power-abuse that have dogged it for so long.

Emerging systems model servant leadership

Given the time spent reflecting on apparently leaderless systems, such as ant colonies and brains, it is valid to ask whether the Emergent Church will have any leadership, and what form that might take. I believe the answer lies in the essential and mysterious free will that sets us apart from other organisms. The ant and slime mold mentioned earlier do not appear to have much choice about their lot. One doesn't find lazy ants who don't pull their weight but sit around sponging off others, or slime mold cells deciding that they can't be bothered to coalesce with the rest. Self-organizing they may be, but that self-organization does not necessarily mean they are freethinking; their environment entirely controls their decisions.

Humankind's journey has been one of flight from the pressures of the environment. We have learned to refrigerate food, develop agriculture, and domesticate animals and thus escape the constant battle to find food to survive. We have learned to build sophisticated shelters and fabrics to protect us from the changes in the weather and have built cities that have paved streets and drainage to lift us from the mud and dirt. The end result of this means that we have the freedom to choose to respond to our environment—both culturally and physically—in ways that other species do not, and the flip side of this freedom is, as ever, that some will abuse it. In order to live communally, since time immemorial, we have balanced our innate freedom with a degree of submission to a community leader. The problem is that we have done so rather willingly and been glad to resign our responsibilities to others for a quiet life. So rather than getting round the problem of sorting out those who abuse their freedom by doing nothing, our easy abdication of responsibility to leaders puts us at their mercy, opening the possibility for them to abuse their power and

114

demand our worship. As Aldous Huxley quipped, "So long as men worship the Caesars and Napoleons, Caesars and Napoleons will duly rise and make them miserable."[22]

Any system involving free human beings that requires some degree of organization must involve some form of leadership. We have already discussed that anarchy is no better for us than dictatorship, but there has to be a place between these two extremes where leadership can be effective without being abusive. The advantage of complexity theory is that it provides us with a model of leadership that has very little *power*, and this naturally fits very well with the Christian tradition of servant leadership (see Mark 10:43)—a term that appears to have been adopted from the Gospels by complexity theorists.

Keith Morrison states that the role of leaders in an emergent system should be to "change the perceptions of a situation."[23] This is very different from stating what changes ought to be made and telling everyone what the new deal is. They are not there to announce change but to resource change; to provide environments whereby change can happen naturally from the bottom up, as described above. In practice this will probably mean being able to get some oversight, a sense of the bigger picture, and then enabling links between projects and ventures so that feedback and learning can occur. Or trying to facilitate multiple perspectives on situations to allow people to make informed choices. It is very much a background role, not a foreground one. Rob Malda of Slashdot is a good example. Having seen the problem "from above" as the instigator of the forum, he then created a system that allowed it to progress and learn—a system that importantly did not involve him or need him. He created it and set it free and stepped back, just as Christ did. The leaders in the Emergent Church will not be big names; people behind the scenes rarely are. They, like Christ, will be leaders who don't allow people to "default to the professional," but encourage them to get plugged in and involved. They will need to have the same attitude as Rob Malda and be prepared to resource and create something, and then let it free and step back.

Summary: The Emergent Church Must Exist at the Edge of Chaos

We have seen that emergent systems only evolve in the strange places between anarchy and rigidity, and that specifically they begin to emerge only when they are held at the "edge of chaos." It is this place that the church must aim for as it seeks to become conjunctive. What keeps systems at the *edge* of chaos, in the place of life, and stops them toppling over the edge are background regulatory systems. Where cities or communities are successful, these regulations are mild and simply designed to protect the vulnerable and provide safety nets for people. Where cities or communities break down, they are either overregulated—and the people revolt against the militarism or life is stifled—or underregulated—and the society degenerates into lawlessness. In the Emergent Church there will have to be similar, light-touch regulatory systems.

What regulates the regulations and keeps them light-touch will be effective communication at all levels. The beauty of a bottom-up networked system is that any part of the network can communicate with any other part without having to have that communication mediated by some central hub. Abuses of power set in when people can communicate with each other only through a leader figure who can then very easily "divide and rule."

To summarize: we cannot tell exactly what form the Emergent Church is going to have, as it will evolve in local places under local conditions in different ways. But we have

Table 4.1
Rigid Church, Emergent/Conjunctive Church, Anarchic Church: A Table of Values

Rigid Church	Emergent/Conjunctive Church	Anarchic Church
Dictatorial, hierarchical leadership	Devolved, decentralized, resourcing, servant leadership	No leadership
Inflexible service structure, rigid program	Genuinely flexible structure and program	No structure, no program
Vertical communication, leader acts as main mouthpiece, little meaningful communication between people on the ground	Networked communication, much meaningful communication between people on the ground	No effective communication
Knowledge and truth resides in leader	Distributed knowledge, truth resides in the community	No shared knowledge, no agreed truth
Always look to the past for guidance	Future vision and past tradition enlighten present practice	The future is everything, nothing in the past or present is good enough
People herded	People gather freely	People don't want to gather
Leader controls mechanisms of forgiveness, communion, etc.	Devolved, communal responsibility for forgiveness, communion, etc.	No recognized mechanisms for forgiveness, communion, etc.
Sense of belonging from attendance	Sense of belonging from relationships	No sense of belonging
No feedback possible, leadership controls the agenda without consultation	Constant low-level feedback feeds into the agenda, agreed by the community	Feedback is unregulated, agenda veers off in any direction
No change possible	Incremental, ongoing, *Kaizen* approach to change	Change for change's sake

looked at some of the characteristics that we can expect it to have. By way of drawing some of this together, table 4.1 is an attempt to look at various aspects of familiar church life, consider what the extremes of the spectrum are, and suggest what being at the "edge of chaos" might mean for each.

Part 2

Cities

/ Gift /

Dirt

-------5.

{ Cities }

Having gone into some detail about what characteristics the Emergent Church might have, I want to return to the Christ-narrative. As previously mentioned, the context in which we are going to play out this narrative is increasingly urban. People talk of the "global village," as if somehow technological progress has made our urbanizing world more like a small collective of farms. I think this has rarely been people's actual experience; in fact, it has been more the case that the life of the city has infected the village. The cultural theorist Arjen Mulder has, tongue firmly in cheek, said that "wherever your mobile [cell phone] works is the city, and anywhere else is the countryside."[1] And in a sense I think he is right: it is the city that has reached out and infiltrated every part of country life, from mobile phones to Internet shopping, twenty-four-hour news, and celebrity gossip.

I believe that this is no coincidence. The long-story of our faith is from a garden to a city, and as we will see,

Christ's own vector is definitely toward Jerusalem. Why is this, and what does it mean for us? I believe that the city—both in our modern world and in Scripture—stands as the best picture of all that is wrong and right with humanity, precisely because it is in cities that engagement with "the other" is unavoidable. In the city we have no choice but to accept that all options are open: there are all races, all creeds, all faiths, all musics, all cuisines. This is why in our imperfection we find it can be a tense place, and this is why in God's perfection the city—this wild collaboration and co-creation between humanity and divinity—is the metaphor for our final destination.

So, while I understand that not all readers of this book will be living in cities, nor should they, I am deliberately taking this urban focus. Urbanization has marched on at huge speed over the last centuries, but our theology has not. It has, largely, remained a "pastoral" theology—a theology of the rural church. However, while this is a deliberate attempt to correct the balance, I strongly believe that because of the huge impact cities have on us wherever we are living, we all have much to learn from such a focus. I would invite you, therefore, to take the use of the word *city* in its widest sense in the following chapters. It is the city that speaks of our interconnection. The city that speaks of our brokenness. And it is toward this city that Christ moved.

First, then, given that the place that this Emergent Church is going to increasingly have to minister is in the urban environment, I want to look in more depth at God's evolving attitude to the city, and explore how conjunctivity will be vital to our urban ministry. Second, I want then to take just two aspects of Christ's ministry—gift and dirt—and use them as examples of Christ's own conjunctive outlook, explaining why I think they will need to be reemphasized if the Emergent Church is going to take root in a world where the city is the norm.

122

The Christian story of the city can be traced back to Genesis 4, soon after Adam and Eve tumbled from Eden and, in troubled family isolation, brother killed brother. In one flick of the knife Cain made three cuts, not only killing his brother Abel, but in the same slashing movement rejecting God and poisoning the earth with blood. When challenged by God he then added deceit to murder and so brought down a curse on himself: he would be "driven from the ground, which [had] opened its mouth to receive [Abel's] blood" (v. 11).

God explains that the separation of Cain from the earth was to have two axes. First, the ground would not yield food for him, and second, he was to be a "restless wanderer" (v. 12). Cain recognizes a third dimension himself, proclaiming that under this curse he would be "hidden from [God's] presence" (v. 14). However, his fears that anyone who found him would kill him are allayed by God, who puts a mark of protection on him. He then goes out of God's presence to the land of Nod.

Thus metaphorically separated from the earth and from God, Cain has to construct a new existence from scratch, and he does so by "[lying] with his wife . . . and building a city" (v. 17). This is the origin of the urban species, but an act which all of us will relate to: human hands taking divine soil and building a declaration of independence, a statement of permanence. Told he would be a restless wanderer, Cain constructs an enduring group of residences and, having severed links with his family, he gets about the work of procreation, filling his city with his own kind. So Cain's city becomes the archetype for all our cities, and all our communities—frantically building in some frenzied attempt to escape the curse of loneliness.

In building, Cain is also trying to escape the curse of separation from the earth. Like the precursor to any modern-day city, we can imagine the structures Cain threw up as metaphorically "raised from the ground." We now have pavements and tarmac, drainage and camber, foundations and pilings—all lifting us up from the soil and protecting us from the elements.[2] Cain knew he had poisoned the earth and thus the ground beneath his feet became his enemy: it was to be covered over, sealed under, and strictly controlled. These concrete lids over the free ground were seen by revolutionaries in the Paris of 1968 as signs of urban oppression, of separation from the raw earth that was the symbol of the free spirit. *"Sous les pavés, la plage"* ("Under the cobblestones, the beach") ran one slogan of the Situationist International, and in revolt against the forces that threatened their intellectual, spiritual, and economic freedom, they ripped up the cobblestones, simultaneously revealing the earth beneath and creating missiles from the very materials that symbolized their bondage.

The earth, the soil that exists somewhere under the layers of urban history, is the source of life, the ground from which our life is sustained. By uncovering it these student rebels were reaffirming their rights to live freely from the land. And by covering it Cain was determined to defy God's curse that the ground would not yield for him. We might perhaps pick up a hint of the origins of our modern agriculture here. If Cain was not going to be able to grow food, he would buy it from those who were and import it to his city. We can imagine him and his urban family exchanging their skills for crops, buying in God's blessings from the soil, and thus completing the circle back to Abel's better offering where the whole saga began. Thousands of years later, we city dwellers, descendants of Cain, load our trolleys with exotic fruits and vegetables out of season, in supermarkets with no fields for miles, swapping coins for the earth's bounty without ever having to toil in mud or get our hands dirty. We poison and cover our own earth and exploit others for God's gifts.

With Cain's story, cities do not get off to a very positive start in Scripture. They begin life as statements of everything that is wrong with humanity: violence, damage to the environment, and disregard for God. The trinity of God, creation, and humanity are blown apart, and a city rises on the wasteland that results. And things do not get much better.

Having flooded the earth to wash it clean of evil, God then faces the rise of the city again in Babel. The writer shows us that the tower builders' intentions were very similar to Cain's: "Come, let us build ourselves a city, with a tower that reaches to the heavens, so that we may make a name for ourselves and not be scattered over the face of the whole earth" (Gen. 11:4). God does not like this much. Coming down to see for himself (and God does come over as highly masculine in these early passages), he also notices their unified language. Interestingly, it seems that this is perceived as the real threat—the tower stands simply as a symbol of humanity's urban unity and evident rejection of the need for God's presence to sustain them. Its spires poking at the underbelly of heaven, the tower gives God a wake-up call to the potential of what humanity could do if they continued working together in this way. Seemingly at a loss for how else to change things, Jack Miles's adolescent divinity resorts again to revolution and hits "escape" for a second time: the people are scattered, their language is confused, and they stop their building . . . for a while.

We have seen that this sort of violent action is pretty characteristic of God in Genesis: casting out and cursing, flooding and scattering, circumcising and bartering over the destruction of Sodom. And like all revolutionary change, its effects are not transformative. People are scattered but continue to build cities. Languages are confused, but people still travel and communicate and share stories and myths. Just as the flood failed to flush out evil, so the scattering of the Babel-onians failed to stop humanity's attempts to build their Utopias east of Eden. If God wanted to transform his creation, then he couldn't continue periodically pressing "reset." A different mode of change was required if the problem of the city was to be dealt with.

Jump forward an undisclosed period of time to a hotel room in New York City, where an African American reporter from the *New York Times* is questioning the theologian Matthew Fox on the relevance of his "creation spirituality" to her thoroughly inner-city roots. He asks her to look out of the window and describe what she sees: bricks. He continues to question: what are bricks? Just clay hoisted hundreds of feet by humans, supported by frameworks of steel mined from the earth, with cars below running on rubber tires, burning fuel distilled from the residue of dead plants from millions of years ago. He goes on, trying to get her to see the essential naturalness in the city, and concludes: "A city—as awesome a place as it is—is also earth, earth recycled by humans who themselves are earth standing on two legs with moveable thumbs and immense imaginations."[3]

Regardless of the controversy surrounding some of his other writings, this is a stunning insight; one which I believe helps us to unlock God's evolving attitude to the city. And clearly it must have evolved, for between Genesis and Revelation God somehow becomes city-positive. At some point God sees that a policy of continually trashing the cities his creations are building is not going to work. Not only that, but God begins to love the city, to be upbeat about it, and having begun in the plains and fields of Genesis, Scripture ends up with the wonderful description of the Holy City, where the dwelling of God is with humanity, and God will live with them (see Rev. 21:3).

The city started life as a statement of independence from God, but it ends up expressing perfectly the goal of divine and human cohabitation. The power of Fox's insight is that the division between the municipal and the rural is a totally false one, and in his conjunctive view of the city, he sees that everything that we have in it is made from the raw materials of the earth. In *A Thousand Years of Nonlinear History*, Manuel de Landa goes beyond this. Though he does not suggest God's hand in it, he sees the emergence of bone in the organic world as the definitive moment that "made new forms of movement control possible among animals, freeing them from many constraints, and literally setting them into motion to conquer every available niche in the air, in water, and on land"[4]—which we might parallel with God's commission to "fill the earth and subdue it" (Gen. 1:28). He then suggests that the invention of bricks and the emergence of the city—which he calls "the urban exoskeleton"—performed a parallel function in the development of human society, allowing it to experience new levels of motion control, with trade, news, food, and goods all traveling in new ways because of it. Hence we might see that our act of creating cities was in fact an imitation of God's act of creation—breathing life and bones into matter to command new levels of control—and if this is the case, then God's desire to end history in urban cohabitation with us is a profound affirmation of our roles as creators, created in God's image. God sees what we have made, and is pleased with it.

In building cities, human hands have taken divine materials and worked them to create new ones. Thus the very fabric of the city is testament to the cooperation between God and humanity. It is a co-creation, a partnership where God has provided the raw materials and we have worked them into fabulous architectural masterpieces full of light and space, allowing the free movement and congregation of people, exchanging ideas and technologies . . . soaring skyscrapers cloaked in glass, brownstone apartment blocks and Manhattan townhouses, expansive docks and arching bridges . . . and slums and tenement blocks and concrete monstrosities and gluttonous penthouses and temples to money and mean streets. In our cities, life's rich tapestry is woven altogether, and it tells the full story of the triumphs and disasters of our urban project. We have built perfect testaments to the human situation: taking God's gifts and simultaneously using and abusing them. Both our divine heritage and rebellious creativity are betrayed in our buildings.

Yet if we truly believe that God is present in the city and that the civic space is going to be the place God finally dwells, then we ought to be able to find hints of God in our cities now. We need to train our ears and eyes to pick up these subtle traces, just as with Fox we need to reimagine the buildings that surround us as reconfigured earth. In many ways the principles of Fowler's stages of faith can be paralleled with our journey as city dwellers. There are those of us at Stage 3, where everything in the city is new and exciting and right—and there will be those who live silk-cushioned and air-conditioned lives in the sterilized "nice" parts of our cities who will never go beyond that. But for most of us who have lived in a city for a while, we go through a Stage 4, where perhaps we are a victim of crime, and the realities of the difficulties come crashing in on us. We either have the option to escape altogether, or cocoon ourselves deeper into our "nice" ghettos and make a note not to venture out again. Or we refuse to give up on the city and refuse to let the city remain unchanged. It takes a long time to commit to a city, but a conjunctive, Stage 5 view of it does come, where we see beyond the mean streets and bad areas and inequality to the deeper issues and the essential goodness. It is only in doing this that the city space can become a spiritual resource for us. The problem is that, just as many people spiritually never get beyond the naïveté of Stage 3, many seem unable to commit to the urban journey to reach the conjunctive view of the city, and resign themselves to the view that it is "godless," talking about having to head to the mountains or oceans and rugged open spaces in order to "find God."

It is undeniable that in the open country—perhaps after Mulder we ought to say "the places our mobiles don't work"—it seems easier to tune in to God and, more importantly, tune out all the noise of the city and its constant hum of people. This has always been the case. In 1835 the English painter Thomas Cole wrote in his "Essay on American Scenery" that "amid those scenes of solitude from which the hand of nature has never been lifted, the associations are of God the creator—they are his undefiled works, and the mind is cast into the contemplation of eternal things." In his fabulous book *The Art of Travel*, Alain de Botton writes of how from the eighteenth century it became popular for travelers to seek out "sublime" landscapes where they could experience what Cole describes. On his own travels to the Sinai desert, de Botton tries to articulate just what makes the experience of the dawn rising there "sublime":

> What then is this feeling? It is generated by a valley created 400 million years ago, by a granite mountain 2300 metres high and by the erosion of millennia marked on the walls of a succession of steep canyons. Beside all three man seems merely dust postponed: the sublime as an encounter, pleasurable, intoxicating even, with human weakness in the face of the strength, age and size of the universe. . . . The sense of awe may even shade into a desire to worship.[5]

This ability of raw nature to put our own weaknesses and pains into perspective is a valuable one, and we see in Job someone experiencing it in the extreme. Having suffered multiple calamity and loss, Job listens to his friends' advice, but discards it as "proverbs of ashes" and "defenses of clay" (Job 13:12). Answers could not be found from those immediately around him. After all this guff, God finally answers the question of Job's suffering out of a storm:

> Where were you when I laid the earth's foundation?
> Tell me, if you understand.
> Who marked off its dimensions? Surely you know!
> Who stretched a measuring line across it?
> On what were its footings set, or who laid its
>   cornerstone . . . ?
> Who shut up the sea behind doors?
>
> Job 38:4–8

And so it continues for four chapters. Job gets no direct answers to his problem of pain, but in God's tirade of images about the raw power of creation, Job's suffering is put into a new context. As de Botton concludes:

> If the world is unfair or beyond our understanding, sublime places suggest it is not surprising things should be thus . . . Sublime places gently move us to acknowledge limitations that we might otherwise encounter with anxiety or anger in the ordinary flow of events . . . Human life is as overwhelming, but it is the vast spaces of nature that perhaps provide us with the finest, the most respectful reminder of all that exceeds us. If we spend time in them, they may help us to accept more graciously the great unfathomable events that molest our lives and will inevitably return us to dust.[6]

Time spent "in the mountains" is therefore important for us when facing the "big questions." In the presence of raw creation, untouched by human hands, clear channels of communication seem to open up and we hear God's assurances clearly. However, the messages that we hear from God in these sublime places are similarly raw and straightforward: *I love you . . . It's OK . . . I exist.* These are important messages to hear from time to time, but they do not deal with the day-to-day complexities of life on the ground in the city.

William Wordsworth wrote much of his poetry almost as an aid to tolerating city life, considering his lines as daily doses of natural images that he believed improved his character and helped him resist the rat race of urban anxieties:

> If, mingling with the world, I am content
> With my own modest pleasure, and have lived
> With God and Nature communing, remov'd
> From little enmities and low desires,
> The gift is yours. . . .
> Ye mountains! thine, O Nature! Thou hast fed
> My lofty speculations; and in thee
> For this uneasy heart of ours I find
> A never-failing principle of joy
> And purest passion.[7]

My trouble with Wordsworth's response to the problems of living in the city is that his poetry is an attempt to "remove" himself personally from it. If our only answer to the obvious pain, greed, and ugliness that the city presents to us on a daily basis is to remove ourselves, then there is no hope for improvement. One sees modern-day Wordsworths—plugged into headphones providing intravenous classical music, while beggars shake tins unheard; or sitting aloof in swathes of leather, high above the dirty pavements in SUVs, as pedestrians choke and traffic jams . . . This is not so much "passing by on the other side" as lifting into the air and floating over. They have solved the problems for themselves alone, and seem disinterested in getting involved in wider solutions.

In a similar way, if we listen for God only in the mountains, we will hear only simple words and personal solutions.

If we are really to engage with and tackle the problems that the city presents to us every day, it is my belief that we need to take the time to listen for God in the city. If Matthew Fox is right, then by tuning in to the city we will begin to hear the message not of God alone but of God's full and mature incarnate complexity, of divinity and humanity in cooperation. These are not me-and-God platitudes but rich communications involving the whole spectrum of humanity, the people I work with, the troubles and doubts and rushes and struggles and highs and lows and crimes and injustices, messages about how God is working toward sanctifying and integrating all of this through us. Escaping to the countryside may be the place to work out the personal, the individual aspects of our spirituality, but the city is the place where we need to be working out our corporate life, for it is this work of preparation of the "holy city" that God is interested in, above our own introspective holiness trip.

Our destiny is not a quiet place with just God and us in some high plains ranch. As Meister Eckhart advises,

> Spirituality is not to be learned in flight from the world, by fleeing from things to a place of solitude; rather we must learn to maintain an inner solitude regardless of where we are or who we are with. We must learn to penetrate things, and find God there.[8]

We must learn to penetrate our communities and penetrate our workplaces. We must learn to penetrate our cities and find God in them. These connected, complex places are where it will not be God alone, but God and us and him and her and white and black and rich and poor and illiterate and abused and gay and straight and Protestant and Catholic and the whole feast of life. And only in the city can we get that message. It is not an easy message to tune into with so much white noise and hatred and difficulty and screwed-up transport and mugging and division . . . But with practice, with a commitment to engaging positively with the city and looking to catch it doing good rather than always on the lookout to knock it down, we can begin to see glimpses of why God is committed to the city as our future: because the redeemed city is the final expression of humanity and divinity in cooperation. It is the conjunction of God's creation with our creativity, where we are building something together. In pursuit of this, I prefer Merwin's response to Wordsworth's:

Thanks

Listen
with the night falling we are saying thank you
we are stopping on the bridge to bow from the
    railings
we are running out of the glass rooms
with our mouths full of food to look at the sky
and say thank you we are standing by the water
    looking out
in different directions

back from a series of hospitals back from a
    mugging
after funerals we are saying thank you
after news of the dead
whether or not we knew them we are saying thank
    you
in a culture up to its chin in shame
living in the stench it has chosen we are saying
    thank you

over telephones we are saying thank you
in doorways and in the backs of cars and in
    elevators
remembering wars and the police at the back door

and the beatings on the stairs we are saying thank
    you
in the banks that use us we are saying thank you
with the crooks in the office with the rich and the
    fashionable
unchanged we go on saying thank you thank you

with the animals dying around us
our lost feelings we are saying thank you
with the forests falling faster than the minutes
of our lives we are saying thank you
with the words going out like cells of a brain
with the cities growing faster over us like the earth
we are saying thank you faster and faster
with nobody listening we are saying thank you
we are saying thank you thank you and waving
dark though it is.

                           W. S. Merwin[9]

If somewhere along the line God became "city-positive,"
then I believe that it is Christ's incarnation and subsequent
ministry and passion that are the clearest signs of that
changed attitude. In them we see the emergence of a new
way of approaching the problem of the historical city as
the place of rebellion against God.

Perhaps the word *approach* is exactly the right one, for
the mode of Christ's physical approach seems to suggest
in itself a different way of dealing with the city than the
rather rampant and violent way the beginnings of the Old
Testament show us. This is no prophet whose immediate
urge is to get into the city, into the main thoroughfares
and meeting places, and make huge announcements and
slamming indictments. On the contrary, although Christ
approaches the city deliberately, he does so slowly, gently,
and carefully. At a young age we know he had been taken
to Jerusalem by his parents and was clearly comfortable in

those surroundings, yet it is in the desert after his baptism that we first get a sense of his attitude toward it.

In the series of three vignettes in the temptations passages (see Matt. 4:1–11) we see another example of the necessity of waiting before change can occur. Even after the drama of his baptism, with God appearing to confirm his status in the descending dove, Christ does not just get "straight to it" but heads into the desert.

One can read these temptations passages as a battle between old and new modes of ministry. Was Christ going to default to the Old Testament ways of revolution or begin a new era of spiritual evolution? There were clearly many options open to him, and it was vitally important that he got it right. In these passages, where the conflict between above and below is so pronounced, it is tempting to over-emphasize Christ's divinity and forget his full humanity. It is too easy to see him as the powerful Messiah, doing away with Satan with snappy ripostes to his testing questions. We ought instead to appreciate here more than anywhere his frail humanity: he had to make the right decisions; he had to face these genuine temptations to do things differently, and to do this required a mind so focused that he went without food for forty days. In reading we are looking into the inner turmoil of God, tempted to revert to change by revolution—to go back to his violent adolescent past and go charging in to put things right . . . but this God is now tempered by a fragile human heart, understanding and empathizing more completely than before the human condition, the difficulties and complexities, the pain and condemnation of the Law and the need for a new way. We are looking in on Christ's own journey toward conjunctivity and beyond.

He is first tempted to turn stones into bread. What better way to spark a wave of interest, a stampede of support, than with this miraculous provision. Follow me and you'll never need be hungry again! Free bread for life! No more work or toiling in the fields, no more worries about seasons or droughts or the world around you, because when stones can be turned into food, we can all be satisfied and never be in need again. People want, and people want it easy—and this stunt would play the people right into his hands via their most basic desires . . . But true love is not easy, and relationships need work. Salvation is not an economic offer, an escape from the rat race. It is beyond selling or buying and won't be received just because a stomach is full. Offers of something for nothing, bread from stones, riches overnight, $2,000 a week tax free for part-time work, immediate weight loss while you eat what you like—all these great scams cry out to us daily in the city from lamppost stickers and billboards and infomercials, playing on our innate desire to leave work behind and enter the lazy nirvana of the lottery winner. But Christ knows that this is no way to bring people to God. They must choose to love, and we must resist the temptation to violate that free choice with dressy claims of cheap salvation.

Christ is then tempted to go to Jerusalem and climb to the highest point of the temple—the metaphorical center and focal point of the whole city—and from there to fling himself down and be caught by a squadron of angels. A huge publicity coup, a demonstration of enormous power—this would be a guaranteed way to stun the city into noticing him, to whip up a froth of excitement and chatter . . . start a godly revolution! Christ knows that, as in Debord's *Society of the Spectacle*, the city could be also won over with tricks and fantastica. He could wow the crowds and gain their admiration . . . but how to keep them? The city is easily bored and needs new distractions and ever more wonderful displays—jumping off the temple once would be great, but to top that and hold them he would need to do more and more and more: forget the

136

spiritual stuff, show us a trick—do something amazing! Love will not be stunned into us, and we must resist the temptation to make church a spectacle, to put on visual feasts or sensational healings and blow people's minds and lead them thus mindless into the pews.

Finally Christ is shown "all the kingdoms of the world and their splendor." This is a different tack—the temptation is not so much to make the mission easier but to give it up altogether and settle for an easy life. Again, we must not underestimate Christ's genuine humanity and freedom of choice; this option was open to him. The city has the rich wares and splendor of the whole world on display on our doorstep. In many of our homes sit Internet connections: portals to an infinite array of desires, passions, and wants as well as instant information about the plight of anything anytime. We are overloaded and fragmented by this display. Our eyes can hardly escape the advertisements wherever we choose to gaze or walk; our field of vision has been sliced up and sold off, our earshot is crammed full of messages about what we need and what we should want to want. It is a blitz of shocking intensity.

In the transcripts of his talks on contemplation at the Abbey of Gethsemani, Thomas Merton talks about the thesis of the German-born American political philosopher Herbert Marcuse, which criticizes modern industrial society as "one dimensional." Merton explains that in such a society

> everything is reduced to the lowest common denominator and everybody fits into that. Things are organized so you can fit in easily and happily. The person who fits in painlessly, who does all the approved things . . . watches all the approved programs . . . is "one dimensional." When everybody fits into this mold, then everything will work smoothly, everyone will make lots of money, the GNP will

go up, everybody will pay their taxes, blacks will keep their mouths shut and we will win all our wars.[10]

In this one-dimensional world, freedom is an illusion. We are free to have any color or model of car we like—but have a car we must. We are expected to have views on which brands we like, but no views on religion. Marcuse argues that the dominant power structures are able to construct and then keep the lid on such a society, keep everybody conforming and uncritical, by perpetuating three lies. The first lie is that things are too big, too complicated, and too advanced for any sort of change to be possible. "We can't change the system now, because it's gone too far." The second is that if you do try to change things, you will pay the price financially—you will be worse off and won't be able to enjoy your current quality of life. And the third is that if you *do* step out of line, people will mock you and laugh at you. Thus we are kept in one-dimensional bliss, unable to see the truth just beyond us in solid space that things are not right and we are being exploited by the powerful.

It will come as no surprise to learn that many reviewers saw the Wackowski brothers' *Matrix* films as heavily influenced by Marcuse's work. Others have seen the central character, Neo, as a type of Christ figure. What is interesting to note as a quick aside is how Christ and Neo compare in their attempts to break people out of their one-dimensional captivity into multidimensional conjunctivity. Both perhaps start with the same idea that freedom begins, as Merton says, "not by telling slaves to be free, but by telling people who *think* they're free that they're slaves." However, their chosen routes from then on diverge quickly. Neo's solution is the classic Hollywood one of redemption through violence: *Matrix Revolutions* indeed. It is guns and bullets and war and fighting that will solve this problem and save the world. This contrasts to Christ's refusal to fight the system.

138

He would not be made a Zealot. He works a redemption which suffers violence but refuses to use it, thus breaking the cycle of retaliatory bloodshed that is the curse of so many conflicts.

Having failed to win Christ over to the way of revolution, of using shock and awe tactics and thus violating their freedom to choose, Satan's third temptation is to ask him, "Why bother?" It is the temptation to remain in the first dimension, not to rock the boat and not fall out of line. One can imagine Christ wondering if change was possible at all: surely he was too small to make any difference. And then thinking of the price he would pay and the abuse he would have to suffer. All of these forces that keep us in check and stop us from talking to each other on the subway, helping the homeless and making a stand—they all attempted to rein Christ in and stop him making the decision to accept his mission.

He was tempted to try the commercial line and feed everyone with bread, to try the celebrity line and stun the crowds with spectacular tricks, and to just give up. And like Christ we face those temptations—perhaps more in the urban church than elsewhere. And like Christ we must resist. We must show, like him, the miracle of restraint— shunning displays of might and power, stepping away from ideas of revolution, and avoiding those who say nothing will change. Christ stepped away from the desert as a divinity determined to do things differently. God had turned away from violent revolution—in Christ he would approach the city in a new way, refusing to rain down plagues and march round its walls.

He knew that the city would resist him—that it still stood as a symbol of rebellion and self-sufficiency. That the priests in power and the money changers in cahoots would not stand for his message of God and humanity cooperating in a holy city that had no need for a temple (see Rev. 21:22).

But he had to go. His whole ministry was evolving toward this finale: God's humble approach to the place humanity built in defiance of him, asking to be allowed in, like a parent approaching the room to which they sent their child in a flash of anger . . . Gently knocking.

Of course, we celebrated initially, thinking we had won some moral victory, and laid down palms and shouted in the streets. But soon it became clear that this was no abdication, no admission of guilt. Yes, he had come to us, but not to furnish our rebellion with legitimacy. And seeing this, the celebration turned to outrage, the shouts of joy to screams of crucifixion . . . Expelled like a foreign body, the organism of the city took Christ to a hill outside its walls and finally got rid of him. Cain's creation took up the knife and once more spilt blood, poisoned the ground, and severed relationships . . . The "urban exoskeleton" exposed and broke the bones of God.

Or did it? What they could not see when they split his skin was their weapons simultaneously ripping the curtain in the temple, pulling down the screen that had kept God boxed up, pigeonholed, controlled, and regulated. What they could not see was that rather than finally putting to death this God who had cast them out, they had inadvertently catalyzed Christ's full emergence.

We will return to the issue of Christ's "emergence" in chapter 8. For now I want to focus on the fact that Christ's attitude to the emerging city was not one of antagonism or annihilation. Quite the opposite. Christ approached the city in order to become a part of it, to infect it, to plant some seed within it that he hoped would take root and grow, drawing the city toward its fulfilled state: that of the place of divine and human cohabitation. This is not where our cities are now, but it is where they are destined to go. And for this reason we must not give up on them. Difficult as it is going to be, we must not abandon our cities or barricade ourselves into sanitized parts of them. If we are not going to face their troubles and stay around to try to improve them, who is? We must learn to appreciate that the very fact that there is pain in our cities is why they are so vital. The city is the place where we are forced to meet with and journey with "the other": the drunkard, the asylum seeker, the lonely, the homeless; it is a multicultural melting pot—all of humanity is here. So we must stay and celebrate these things and try to make them work because this is what the destiny of the city is: to be a place where we can all live together.

As if echoing Fowler's admission that Stage 5 is only reached through the pain of Stage 4, Richard Sennett concludes his book *Flesh and Stone* by saying that the very thing that binds a city together into a community is the shared experience of difficulty and suffering, and only a city that has experienced that will be a compassionate place. The city will thus become conjunctive, become a place that can empathize with pain,

> only if it acknowledges that there is no remedy for its suf-
> ferings in the contrivings of society, that its unhappiness
> has come from elsewhere, that its pain derives from God's
> command to live together as exiles.[11]

Having created the city out of Cain's painful rejection, humanity must come to terms with the fact that pain will remain in the city until God fully becomes part of it. There is no perfect planning configuration that will solve the problems we have in our cities, towns, and villages, and no amount of razing and redesigning will make them trouble free. Discussing the designing and rebuilding of Paris after the violence and oppression of the times leading up to and through the French Revolution, Sennett remarks that the "revolutionaries believed that . . . pain could be erased by erasing place";[12] as the later student revolutionaries of 1968 testified with their ripping up of the pavements, it could not then, and it cannot now. Christ had to come to be wounded by the city precisely because the city is the place where wounds are carried, where pain cannot be hidden, where people have to face their prejudices, their hatreds, their fears. But he also had to come to the city because it was the melting pot of cultures and ideas, and therefore the forge for outrageous creativity: music, theater, clubs, galleries, bars, comedy, opera, discussions, lectures . . . listings and listings of creative talent on show. The Creator had to come to the focus of creativity and celebrate it with us. The God who created the bones that allowed us to move had to come to the "urban exoskeleton" we had constructed, and affirm our status as co-creators.

For these reasons we are compelled to carry on the work Christ started, not scared off by those who claim religious power or have vested interests in the dominant modes of being. The city is the place where our dreamy theologies must get their hands dirty and work themselves out in praxis. The temptations will be there to attempt revolution, to pour resources into big projects and top-down structures, to try to impress people with our power and sell them salvation in exchange for needs met. It will also be tempting to do nothing, to say that everything is too big, too complicated for us to change; to retreat to the suburbs, or even to the country, where things will be easier. We will be told that if we do attempt change we will lose out and people will mock. We must ignore these one-dimensional messages. As Oliver Wendell Holmes wrote:

> The chief worth of civilization is just that it makes the means of living more complex; that it calls for great and combined intellectual efforts, instead of simple, uncoordinated ones, in order that the crowd may be fed and clothed and housed and moved.[13]

It is to this complex task in the city that the church is called. We must give ourselves humbly, give birth to new forms and organisms, allow the church to emerge and adapt, to work its way through streets and subways, drawing, as the city always has, on God's created resources, working them with our hands, bringing our own creativity and technology to bear on them, not for our own glory, not to state our independence, but for the glory of God, for justice and equality, for celebration and unity. We are the community of the Creator, so we must create. We are the community that looks forward to the city where divinity and humanity will live side by side, so we must give birth to an emergent, conjunctive, self-renewing, adaptable church that can model this in inclusivity, generosity, creativity, and flexibility, welcoming the Other, providing true space for pain, and real time for carnival.

6.

{ Gift }

Christ began his journey to embrace the city in the desert, where he rejected the crude transactionalism of those who would tempt him to seek devotees through stunts and bread. He turned away from a style of ministry that tried either to get people to exchange their commitment for the meeting of their material needs or wow them into belief through displays of power and magic. Christ did this because he had dedicated himself to a new way, to a conjunctive approach to the city. Gone were the times of Joshua when battles would be fought and infidels put to the sword, and the times of Elisha and Elijah when bears attacked hecklers and God proved points by sending soaking piles of wood up in flames. There would be healings, but no sideshow.

However, it is clear that, despite resisting these trades, there was some kind of transaction occurring in Christ's ministry, just as there is in the church's ministry today. Something is given, and something is received. It is vital that we, like Christ, get the nature of this exchange right, for we risk ending up as another product to buy or sensation to seek unless we do. Graham Cray is wise to note that "the dominance of consumerism presents a major challenge to Christian faithfulness,"[1] a concept brilliantly explored in Alain de Botton's book *Status Anxiety*.[2] As we move from our localized peaks and seek out higher ground, I want in this chapter to suggest that a conjunctive approach to faith must reevaluate the church's modes of exchange, and that central to our critique of consumerism must be the rediscovery of the transaction of gift.

About five years ago in the Vaux community, we began to explore the nature of this transaction as we thought more about the kinds of events and services we were putting on, and how people were responding to them. Were we simply part of the "service industry" that has grown up alongside the alternative worship movement, supplying liturgies and video loops and ambient sounds to furnish the spiritual apartments of those who wandered our way from the traditional church? What was going on when we worshipped anyway? People in churches I had attended spoke about "enjoying" a time of worship and getting a lot out of it. Did they just mean they liked the songs and it made them feel warm inside? And were we just offering the same core product in a different style of packaging?

Many of our answers to these questions were fed by the resurfacing of a work by the American writer Lewis Hyde. *The Gift* is a book about art and what art is "worth." In it, Hyde proposes that there are two possible modes of exchange. One is market exchange, where goods or currency are swapped, and the other is by gift, for which no money or goods are necessarily reciprocated immediately. In a market exchange the scales are always balanced by payment and there is an essential equilibrium. But with a gift there is constant movement from body to body, a momentum as the gift is passed from hand to hand. As Hyde says, "The gift that cannot be given away ceases to be a gift."[3]

The distinction between market exchange and gift is highlighted by the difference between going to a restaurant to eat and having people over for dinner. At the restaurant there is money exchanged for the food and drink provided, and so there is an equilibrium created by the payment— nobody owes anybody anything. At the dinner party, no money is offered or exchanged—indeed to do so would be incredibly rude. The food is a gift, passed freely from the host to the guests. As a gift it has created a momentum, a disequilibrium, and it would be expected—although never demanded—that the guests might in the future reciprocate the gift in some way.

We can see then that with gift exchange there is always a latency or potentiality for relationship, whereas with market exchange everything is clearly balanced and there is no relational potential. Not that this is always a bad thing. Many of us enjoy the blandness and clinical nature of the supermarket simply because it allows us to practice pure market exchange: we hardly even need speak to the cashier. Living in cities that can fragment us with their myriad daily interactions, the opportunity to shop without a long conversation about Betty's corns or the weather, when all we really want is our bacon and milk, can be welcome.

Hyde's thesis is that true works of art function as transforming, life-giving gifts, yet exist simultaneously in these two economies of market exchange and gift. Art can be bought and sold for a profit, but in its essence, it is gift. Indeed, Hyde proposes that "a work of art can survive without the market, but where there is no gift there is no art."[4] True art presents itself to us as a gift that can aid transformation, an antidote to the restless death of the commodity civilization; but it is a delicate gift, whose power can be destroyed very easily if it is turned into pure commodity. (One might reflect on the mass production of Matisse's work as posters for sale in every poster shop on every Main Street and find truth in Hyde's words: the force of the pieces has been lost, their soul destroyed.)

At a basic level then, we might reflect on the extent to which our practices in church function as commodity or gift. I recently heard of a church that had been invited by a "mission agency" to participate in an evangelism program with other churches in its area. The idea was to hand out free hamburgers to shoppers in the town center, and for people from the churches to be around to sit and strike up conversations with them on the picnic tables around. The agency proposed that this work would cost this one church £3,000 (over $5000), but that as it was more wealthy than some of the other churches in the area, it ought to give £6,000 (over $10,000), which it did. On the surface, it appeared that the churches were participating in a gift transaction that ought to carry with it the potential for good relationships. However, it turned out to be a disaster. Only one or two people were drawn into the church as a result, and both of them had previously been committed churchgoers. A lot of precious resources had been spent, and many in the church felt they had been "had."

I would suggest that the reason this was a disastrous venture was precisely because most of the transactions involved were of the wrong sort. First, the churches were literally buying into a program, and that inevitably meant that their relationship to it was as commodity, not gift. They paid their money, and expected a good return on it. Second, handing out gifts of free hamburgers in the town center obviously created a great deal of resentment from the other people there, who were trying to make a living by selling hamburgers as commodities. The churches were actually in danger of putting people out of business. Third, if the church was going to insist on handing out free food, it could perhaps have done better than greasy, unhealthy burgers that are the product of intensive farming techniques and are pumped full of additives. Their gifts lacked integrity. Fourth—and most seriously—as discussed in the last chapter, the principle of using gifts as a way of starting conversations about faith is one that Christ rejected, and we should too. Not that we should close all soup kitchens; it is just that they must not be used as a means to a different end, but as an end in themselves.

We must clearly be very careful about our gift practice in the context of faith, and ensure that we get the distinction between appropriate commodity transaction and appropriate gift transaction. To blur the line between the two is likely to cause all sorts of problems and lead to allegations of manipulation.[5]

On reading *The Gift* for the first time, it was clear that there were many lessons like this to draw from it for our own experience in Vaux. On the most basic level, where one read "art," one can read "worship." Much of my experience of worship in traditional churches, especially in the "renewed" wings, was that it was judged on a subjective level by what people got out of it, not what they put in. "That was a good time of worship—I really got a lot from it" was a very common comment on Sunday at 9 p.m. after the service in the local pub. I only really considered this attitude when, having been working on Vaux for a while, I realized that I was not "getting much out of" the services and I became worried by the question of whether I was "worshipping" at all. What Hyde's book helped me to realize was that if worship is a gift, then it is absolutely not about what I am looking to get out of it, but what I am looking to give. Churches must steer clear of "selling worship," as if it could be remarketed and rebranded through some surface pick-and-mix of popular culture. Who am I to come to worship the Almighty and expect to get something? Yet that's what most of us do, turning up tired from the week's work and busy weekend, needing our batteries recharged, looking for a bit of a power pack from God or to be caught up in some holy moment.

Having been refreshed by these simple truths, deeper reading on gifts revealed that their movement and cycles are more sophisticated. Gifts are very rarely just two-way affairs where I give to you and you give back to me, nor are they limited to periods of transition. The problem is that the gift-practice the church is known for seems to be limited to these narrow ideas. People come to church to celebrate their transitions with baptisms, confirmations, weddings, and funerals—and even these are becoming less and less common. It is my belief that if we are going to see an Emergent Church, we must reevaluate our gift-practice, make it less narrow and more complex. Most cultures traditionally have quite complex gift cycles operating in them, which Hyde discusses in some depth in his book. I want to look at one in particular from the Maori tribes of New Zealand, which has three gifts within it, and then reflect on how these three gifts might prove instructive to us as we seek to reimagine the church as a place characterized by gift. Hyde describes the Maori hunting ritual in this way:

> The Maori have a word, *hau*, which translates as "spirit," particularly the spirit of the gift and the spirit of the forest which gives food. In these tribes, when hunters return from the forest with birds they have killed, they give a portion of the kill to the priests, who, in turn, cook the birds at a sacred fire. The priests eat a few of them and then prepare a sort of talisman, the *mauri* which is the physical embodiment of the forest *hau*. This *mauri* is a gift the priests give back to the forest, where it "causes the birds to be abundant."[6]

In this hunting ritual the "circle of gift" has been enlarged beyond a two-way exchange between forest and hunter. The forest "gives" the birds to the hunters, but the hunters are not the ones who return a gift to the forest. Instead, they make a gift of some of the catch to the priests, and it is the priests who then make an offering back to the forest. As Hyde comments:

> With a simple give-and-take, the hunters may begin to think of the forest as a place to turn a profit. But with the priests involved, the gift must leave the hunter's sight before it returns to the woods.[7]

First, this tells us that there is something inherently important about gifts "disappearing" from our sight before they are returned in some form. In this case this is achieved with a third party, but we can see that even when two are involved it is important to "hide" the gift in some way temporarily as it is given—which is why we wrap up presents rather than give them open, and why people on reality makeover shows have to close their eyes before the "reveal."

Second, the third party stops the gift process from straying into commodity exchange (birds taken, offerings given, more birds available, profit made). No party involved receives a gift from the same party that it gave a gift to, so the linkage that would promote profit is broken. The story is told in India of two Hindu women who, in order to deal with their alms-giving duty, decided to give alms back and forth to each other. The story goes that when they died, they were reincarnated as two wells whose water was so bitter that nobody could drink from them. It is only as the circle is expanded to include "the other" that we can be refreshed by gifts.

This Maori ritual can be considered from an environmental angle. The cycle we see here of humanity drawing from nature, offering gifts to the gods, and giving back to nature is, in its fullest sense, a vital one. Our view of creation as a commodity to be exchanged and profited from has impoverished the earth and poisoned it. We teeter at the edge of environmental disaster because of our failure to see creation as a gift. This failure is, in the sense of the Maori example, akin to taking the birds from the forest and selling them all at a profit, with which we buy bigger weapons to shoot more birds. It is a failure to see conjunctively, a failure to appreciate the connectedness of our lives with the life of the planet we inhabit; that if we take without giving back, we destroy the gift.

In our complex, modern society, it is too easy to see creation as a commodity because our horizons are shortened and we cannot see the repercussions of our actions. We burn fuel in our cars, but don't see the acid rain or ravaged oil fields. We buy bananas all the year round, but fail to notice the thousands of miles and energy-heavy cold storage required to get them to us, nor the poor wages and conditions of those forced to pick them—the commodification of humanity . . .

In the Emergent Church we must radically realign ourselves with the environmental movement, not because we are intrinsically antiglobalization (which we might be) or because we want to stop global warming (which we must), but because as Christians we believe that creation is a gift, not a commodity. If it has been given to us as a gift to pass on, it is not ours to do with as we please. It is not ours to dig up, saw down, harpoon, exploit, dynamite, poison, genetically modify, or factory-farm. That we have done so is the result of our disconnection from creation and our commodification of its gifts. And that the church has done so is the result of an escapist view of the day of reckoning, that nothing we do really matters because God will make it all right in the future anyway.

Perhaps the single most positive thing that has happened to the church in the last twenty years is its support of the Jubilee 2000 "Drop the Debt" campaign. That the country was made fully aware that there was a huge and real support in the local churches for global justice was in itself a massively positive step toward realigning the public image of the church as a faceless, uncaring, and impotent institution. If we are serious about engaging with the local places we live in, as well as the world we live in, then the Emergent Church will have to be a just church, an energy-efficient church, a place where people can access information and ideas about more just lifestyles. A local Buddhist center in London springs to mind: using a converted local courthouse, they have transformed it into a café, which serves outstanding organic food from locally sourced producers. The café is stuffed full of information about events and issues to do with local politics, the environment, campaigns, and the arts, and is a beautiful, calm place to meet people. The "temple" rooms attached at the back seem a natural extension, nonthreatening and wholly inviting. It is, unsurprisingly, hugely popular.

Returning to the Maori hunting ritual, I want second to consider what it might have to say about the gift-practice of the church as a "worshipping" community. I have already mentioned that I believe we need to reimagine worship as gift and reemphasize our giving rather than receiving. Looking back to the reasons why a number of us started Vaux in the first place, it was because the churches we were part of gave no opportunity for us to give. Sitting in a huge church full to the brim with around six hundred people, mostly in their early twenties, many of them working as actors, writers, directors, producers, graphic artists, and musicians, it seemed extraordinary that unless they were able to preach or play the guitar their gifts were not welcome. There was no space within the normal weekly services for any of these

153

other talents, yet it was these talents that were being put to use in the marketplace week in, week out. Perhaps it was now less surprising that people were coming to church with an attitude of getting rather than giving, because there was no room in the highly structured, highly dictatorial services for their gifts to be given. Reflecting on the hunting ritual, it was as if these expert hunters were being asked to keep their catch to themselves, leave it at home, come to the priests, and sit through a ritual that purported to benefit them but had no connection to their practice.

The circle of gift is broken if people are denied the opportunity to give, but beyond that, if people are required to "give" what is not truly part of them, then the gifts lack any integrity. My experience of church ended up being doubly frustrating: not only was I unable to offer my gifts, but I was forced to offer gifts of "worship" that were not of myself.

Looking back at Cain and Abel, perhaps the difference between their gifts is that one was truly an offering of part of himself and his labor, and one was not. We are told that Cain gave "some of the fruits of the soil," whereas Abel gave "fat portions from some of the firstborn of his flock"; and we might imagine Cain on his way to the offering just picking up whatever was around, while Abel actually gave something that really mattered to him, something of himself. Given God's attitude to each of these gifts, one might conclude that gifts of worship that are not "of ourselves," that lack integrity for us as people, might not be acceptable at all. Unless I am actually bringing something of myself to worship, it might not be worship.

This has been one of the great strengths of the alternative worship movement. It has given people the space to bring something, anything of themselves and present it as worship. Where in the past artists, poets, dancers, writers, musicians, DJs, and actors have been told to sit down and shut up, with alternative worship they have been invited to bring their gifts in abundance.[8] People have often said to me, "Oh, we'd love to do something like Vaux at our church, but we don't have the gifts." When pressed, what they mean is they don't think they would be able to make videos or installations, which entirely misses the point. The only reason we have been strong on visual art and design is that we have had visual artists and designers involved. If they are not around for a particular service, then we don't try to replicate their gifts; we do without.

Alternative worship is not multimedia worship. It is about allowing people to use their gifts so that they can worship with integrity. It would be folly to pretend that, by installing PA systems, video projectors, and screens, and shipping in tea lights by the ton, every church would suddenly be "doing alternative worship." Buying a labyrinth or some ambient music and video loops doesn't get you any closer to the original spirit of the movement, because what Vaux would call "alternative worship" cannot be bought into; it is not about commodity but gift, and gifts must come from those taking part, not be bussed in from outside.

In the Emergent Church, acts of worship will spring from the economy of gift. They will not be products that can be bought or sold, or commodities to be consumed in exchange for some devotion. However, we must not restrict our thoughts on gift to services. Thinking more widely about our cities, they are massively dominated by market exchange—economic beasts driven by capital and profit in ways that small villages once were not. The church would be foolish to try to play the city at this game and boost its "market share," "reposition itself in the market," or "rebrand" its message with modern advertising and marketing methods, for the essence of what we have cannot be bought or sold. It is not to be consumed and is not a lifestyle choice. Its truth will not be fully told by glamorous girls with smiley, pearly teeth, and eight out of ten people who express a preference will not express its depth or pain or richness or sorrow. In the face of the saturating and all-encompassing urban market, which Hyde rightly associates with empty death that leads nowhere, the church must stand as a beacon of generosity, as a hub for gift exchange and all the relational enrichment that brings.

We have already seen that the Emergent Church will be characterized by an "open" rather than "closed" system approach—it will be open to the environment; sensing it, responding to it, and, in turn, shaping it. I am convinced that the best opportunity the church has to interact with its environment is by focusing its activities and communal life around ideas of gift. The hunters in the Maori ritual do not need to be forced to bring their offerings to the priests. It is an essential part of who they are as human beings; a natural response to their knowledge that life itself is a gift. Deep down we all have a need to give and a need to receive freely. We cannot go through life buying and paying for everything, for to do so would leave us empty and soulless.

The problem in the city is that there are very few spaces where gifts can be exchanged. Public spaces are very often heavily regulated so street performers cannot offer us music or artists decorate our pavements. Indeed, street performer sites on the London Underground are now sponsored by a brewery—which has destroyed the vital element of gift in the music and mediated them as products we can buy into or not. We cannot go to art exhibitions, theaters, or gigs without being assaulted by corporate sponsors trying to bathe in the reflected glory of their transforming gifts.[9] The campaigning organization Adbusters and its self-titled magazine have led protests against the commercialization of our public visual space. They argue—rightly in my view— that we should be able to choose to look at advertising, but the huge hoardings in every direction have actually taken that choice away. Our eyesight now comes with commercial interruptions over which we have no power. Malcolm McLaren—perhaps ironically, given his position as the brains behind the "great rock-and-roll scandal"—recently encouraged people to seek refuge in churches because they were the only places left in our cities where there were no advertisements and where demands were not made of us to buy stuff. He was rightly claiming that churches should be places of gift; useless spaces, free of function and not demanding our money.

McLaren's view is clearly rose-tinted, but his aim is true. Churches must aspire to become centers of gift exchange in the broadest sense. They should provide hanging spaces for artists, venues for music of all types, forums for discussions and debates, classes for expectant mothers . . . whatever gifts there are in the local community, the church should be the place where these gifts can be exchanged or shared. I reiterate: this is not just about services or "Christian" activities. This is about engaging with the local environment and having open boundaries. It is about refusing to see this as infection, but encouraging it as cross-fertilization. It is about declaring our interdependence with the locality we find ourselves in.

In the early 1990s I was part of a small team who, having read Laurence Singlehurst's *Sowing, Reaping and Keeping*, decided to start a band night in the converted crypt of our church. We invited bands from the local schools to play, and all their friends to come along and support. It was a huge success. The next time we did it, more and more bands were keen to play, and more and more people wanted to come and watch. The crypt was a heaving mass of young bodies and outrageously loud music . . . and with the crowds came their accessories: cigarettes, illicit alcohol, recreational drugs. The police were called because of the crowds around the streets. What were we to do?

Rather than finish the story and explain what happened, I want you to think about how you might imagine it went on, bearing in mind what we have learned about emergent systems. How would the balance between anarchy and rigidity be achieved? To what extent should things be regulated? Were certain songs and styles of music off-limits? What response should there have been to the drinking and drugs? Would the rest of the church see this as "infection" or "cross-fertilization"? Should the bands be invited to take part in services? How long should the event be allowed to go on, and how could its "success" be measured? What did the church leadership think of it? Was it a failure if the church youth group saw no increase in numbers? How did the youth group feel about these hundreds of people in "their patch"?

Whatever the outcome, what was abundantly clear was that these young people were starved of space to practice their gifts. In a system that seems to default to "no you can't," they were desperate for people to say "yes"; to affirm them and give them space, equipment, time, facilities, and stages. It is important to recognize that what was going on here was an exchange of gifts. It was not the church "patronizing" them; the bands were given a gift of the space and resources, and the church was given a gift of the music. It can be tough accepting the sharp and edgy gifts of the young, but it is vital to their emotional and spiritual development and well-being that, as parents, schools, churches, and societies, we do.

As part of my work as a teacher I oversee a group of around twenty-five sixth-formers (college students). Every half term the whole of the sixth form is brought together for what is known as a "performance session." Groups of students sign up to perform, and it is emceed by students themselves with absolutely no input from staff.

158

For around an hour the group is entertained by bands, solo singing, stand-up comedy, beatbox, escapology . . . the art form is irrelevant; what is vital is that space is given for gifts to be exchanged. We have seen that life exists "at the edge of chaos," and these performance sessions are a clear example of that. It is noisy and feels slightly out of control in a way that makes some staff feel a little uncomfortable. But it is alive. The atmosphere is electric with support for friends performing—wrong notes or forgotten lines are not mocked. In this chaotic exchange of gifts, life breaks out and the educational market economics of academic achievement and competition are swept aside for a time. It is in these unmediated moments—performances, school trips to Six Flags, staff versus student sports matches—that we see the power of the gift to establish relationships that move into richer and deeper areas than the one-dimensional plane of knowledge transfer. It is this, rather than constant examinations, that education is truly about, and we are foolish to allow our system to be hijacked by the marketplace, which litigiously sees trips as too risky and performance sessions a waste of valuable teaching time.

The Emergent Church will be one of the key places in a community where gifts can be exchanged, and as always when gifts are shared, relationships will flourish around these places. We know from the educational example just outlined that it could be "messy" and that it may not always be clear who is in control—but we must remember that this is where life exists. We also know that accusations will come that activities like this are a "waste of time" and not focused on the main goal of getting everyone saved. We must resist this.

Far too much of our time in church services and church activities is "controlled": we are now praying for this, we are now singing this, we are now listening to this talk . . . Every second is accounted for, as if we shall have to present an audit of how efficient our worship was. Oscar Wilde once quipped that "everyone knows the price of everything and the value of nothing"; he understood that gifts cannot be accounted for or attributed a figure to show how valuable they are. They are priceless because of the relational potential that they carry with them.

Perhaps the most pernicious aspect of market exchange is the insistence that everything and everyone must be able to justify their function and contribution to making a profit. If it is not profitable, chop it off, cut it out, resign it, sell it off . . . Nowhere do we see the contrast between the economy of the gift and the economy of the market more clearly than in situations where relationships and people are put on ledgers. The reason Christ rejected the crude transactionalism of those who would tempt him to seek devotees through stunts and bread was that he understood that his ministry was all about gift. He desires to reunite us with God, not to fulfill some function but because he loves us and longs for relationship with us—and true loving relationships are a gift, utterly devoid of function. Ask two young lovers why they love each other and they will probably be able to reel off a list of reasons: he is really fit, she is dead gorgeous, I like the way he dresses, etc. But ask a couple who have been married for fifty years why they love each other and they may not be able to answer. Their love has deepened beyond good looks and presents and all the transitory things that pass with time. Their relationship has gone deeper than functional foundations: it is "use-less," just as true love is useless in the sense that it cannot be boiled down to function, because that would make it conditional upon that function. What is true in our human relationships is also true with God: my relationship with God is useless. It cannot be boiled down to functions of healing or well-being. God's purpose is not even to forgive me and be done with me—God looks beyond that to true love, to completely useless relationship.

Cities / Gift / Dirt

The Emergent Church must allow people to bring their gifts and share them at every level of its ministry. Again, I want to reiterate that we must think beyond the boundaries and structures that we know now. Organizationally and linguistically the concepts of gift and giftedness have been co-opted, so talk of spiritual gifts is narrowly confined to prophecy or speaking in tongues and other "gifts" that are "useful" to the church reaching its "goal." Their use is managed carefully by leaders who are often seen as having the power to decide which gifts are acceptable and where in the hierarchy they stand.

In a recent seminar at Greenbelt arts festival, I was asked by someone in a question-and-answer session on alternative worship how they could set up a service similar to Vaux, "because we just don't have the gifts in our church." There were murmurs of support for this view, so I simply asked people to get into groups of seven or eight and really think about the gifts they had, the skills they could use, and write them down. There was genuine shock at the depth and breadth of gifts people uncovered. I pushed them beyond that to then think of things that were not connected to worship services that they could offer—with the same results. These were people whose idea of *gift* had been stunted and narrowed by years of sitting in pews listening to organs and sermons. They needed to relearn that whenever we give or use our gifts we are mimicking the Giver of all gifts, and the opportunity to share these gifts together is itself a gift that we should share as widely as possible with the whole community. Addressing the problem of "ministering to a rootless generation" such as this, Henri Nouwen wrote in 1975, "I am afraid that in a few decades time the church will be accused of having failed at its most basic task, offering people creative ways to communicate with the source of life."[10] The Emergent Church must work to answer that accusation.

In terms of the Maori hunting ritual, we have seen how it is vital that people are allowed space to offer their gifts: the priests accept whatever they bring. This is not the end of the cycle though: the priests then prepare the birds offered to them and make a gift of them back to the forest. At this point the nature of the gift cycle enters the mysterious, for there is no rational connection between the gift of the priests to the forest and the continued abundance of birds in the forest for the hunters. Of course, this movement of gift into mystery is not limited to the Maoris. We could equally see the same cycle occurring in our own tradition. In Exodus, God tells Moses that the people should bring to the priests offerings for him from whatever gifts they receive from God, whether children, crops, or livestock. The priests are allowed to eat the flesh of the gifts, but the blood is to be sprinkled and the fat burned to give a pleasing aroma back to God. So the gift cycle enters into mystery again, for no direct linkage can be made between the sacrifices made and the continued fertility of the ground and the people.

This "disappearance" of the gift in one part of the cycle is absolutely vital, for it is here that it is refreshed and renewed. As Hyde comments,

> The inclusion of the Lord in the circle changes the ego in which the gift moves in a way like no other addition. It is enlarged beyond the tribal ego and beyond nature. . . . The gift leaves all boundary and circles into mystery.[11]

But this is essential because "anything contained within its own boundary must contain as well its own exhaustion."[12] Gifts that circle round and round in the human plane cannot ultimately satisfy and are destined to become stale with use. At some point there needs to be a refreshment, a reinvigoration of the gift from an external source.

Christ crawled out of the desert defined by one thing: gift. He would not trade bread or stunts for devotion, nor would he accept wealth and power in exchange for his devotion to another, for this was the way of the city, and if the city was to become God's dwelling place, he needed to model the new economy it would depend on for its growth. His ministry was to be a gift to us, with his stories hanging heavy with meaning, but not forcing themselves on us, and those being healed not told to remain quiet. He wandered from the desert through the villages and towns and hills, until he turned to Jerusalem, where he knew he must offer the greatest gift he had: his life. There is no marketplace in Christ's passion. His death is a gift offering that draws us into mystery so that we might be refreshed. Why couldn't he have stayed? As the parable of the talents tells us, the gift that is not used will be lost, whereas the gift that is used is not used up. Whoever gives his life as a gift will find it, but whoever tries to hold on to it will lose it.

If the Emergent Church is to be a center of gift exchange, then it must also be a place where people experience the mystery of Christ's life-gift too, for "whatever we have been given is supposed to be given away."[13] It must be a place where gifts flow freely and are not allowed to collate in stagnant pools where they will die. It must be a place in touch with its environment and able to sense where the empty places are, so that it may give to them. The market always seeks a profit, but the gift seeks out the empty-handed. So let us become the empty-handed church, happy to receive gifts and pass them on into mystery, refusing to hold on to them for our own blessing. Fourteenth-century German mystic Meister Eckhart advised the wise to "borrow empty vessels," and in his last talk before he died suddenly, Thomas Merton said that such begging bowls represent something of the ultimate theological root of belief: that in being open to the gift we are expressing something of our conjunctivity and essential interdependence—on creation for food, on one another for community, and on God for regeneration as the gift goes out of sight into mystery. Out of the interaction of these simple constituents evolves spiritual complexity, and somewhere at the edge of its chaos is the life we seek.

{ Dirt }

Many of the traditional hymns of the church contain wonderful truths, but I hope an exception is the carol that contains the promise that we shall see Christ, not in a lowly stable, but at God's right hand,

> When like stars, his children crowned,
> All in white shall wait around.

Not only would I be disappointed to get to heaven to find I had to spend eternity "waiting around," but I think I would find the pure white robes rather jarring too. To me they smack of the folklore that "cleanliness is next to godliness," still commonly believed to be a quote from Scripture. I am not against personal hygiene in any way; it is just that these images remind me of the square-jawed, all-American, fuzzy-felt Christ in untainted robes, who wandered around stuck to the not-at-all-dusty plains of my childhood Sunday school.

The Conjunctive Church will be a place that has reevaluated its relationship with dirt and moved on from sterilized backgrounds to appreciate the reality that dirt and dust were everywhere around Christ. There were no phosphate-free detergents, no shower gels, no antiperspirants, and certainly no breath fresheners. We'd all love to meet Christ in person . . . It's just that we'd probably force him to take a bath before we did. Of course, his peers would not have seen him as dirty at all; it's just that as times change, so do definitions of what is dirty and clean, and these definitions change from place to place too. For example, there are accounts of the first Europeans meeting the American Indians, and the Europeans being disgusted at the Indians' habit of emptying their nasal passages onto the ground—just as the Indians were disgusted that these people kept their snot in pocket handkerchiefs. "If you like that filth so much," one Indian is recorded as saying, "give me your handkerchief and I will soon fill it for you." There were similar issues when Europeans arrived in other places: the Pacific Islanders could not believe that these people actually emptied their bowels inside their homes, just as the Europeans could not believe these people emptied theirs straight into the sea, and some Africans concluded that the reason these strange white people arrived with such elaborate and excessive clothing was that they wanted to keep their "gases" close to their bodies.

What is defined as dirty or clean then is not as straightforward as we might think. If my shoes are on the dinner table, they are dirty. If the same shoes are in the closet, they could be clean. Same shoes, different places. The pop can in the plowed field is "litter"—it is the dirty object—but if the can is on the supermarket shelf, not only is it clean, but any soil from that plowed field would itself become the dirt.

The same food that was on my dinner plate not a minute ago suddenly becomes untouchable filth if dumped into the trash. Dirt, it seems, is not a fixed idea, but occurs when "matter is out of place" and thus is created as a by-product of our deciding what the right place for things is.[1]

Whenever we create order, or construct a society, we make decisions about what is in or out, what is right or wrong, and thus what is clean or dirty. If we are to keep the world an orderly place, we need to respect these dirt boundaries: don't drop litter, don't empty your bowels in the wrong place, don't eat food that has been discarded. And these dirt boundaries we create exert some sort of social control. By deciding what is clean or dirty in society, we then tend to legislate to punish those who persistently cross the boundaries between them. How our largely secular society now comes to decisions about what is dirt would be an interesting point of debate, but what is of interest to me now is that in most societies, and in ours for the large part of history, it is actually religion that has set the boundaries. Thus our dirt boundaries are also exerting a form of religious control over people—telling them who is in and who is out, what sort of behavior is acceptable and what is not. It is my belief that the Emergent Church will be, as Christ himself was, a force for reevaluating dirt boundaries, and as a result of these reevaluations, become a place of refuge for those who have previously been labelled as "dirty."

Christ may not have been clothed in pure white garments, and may well not have come up to our standards of personal hygiene, but he and the society he lived in were not ambivalent about dirt. The Old Testament had set out dirt boundaries in great detail (see Leviticus 11–15) and the religious leaders of Jesus's day were real sticklers for ensuring everyone abided by them or cleaned themselves up in the right way if they didn't. Truly, this amounted to enormous social control. They were not only in charge of defining what was clean and dirty but also controlled the mechanisms by which cleansing—or forgiveness—might be achieved. Any threat to the dirt boundaries was therefore a very serious matter that challenged the temple system and, by association, the Almighty himself. So to see this Jesus, who purported to be a prophet and wise leader, stepping over the boundaries left, right, and center, would have been profoundly shocking.

In Matthew 8 we see Christ healing a man with leprosy. Lepers were definitely unclean: they had to ring bells to warn others they were there so no one would risk being infected by touching them. But Christ "reached out his hand and touched" him, and in commanding him to "be clean," it is as if part of his healing was to simply be touched and told, "You *are* clean" (vv. 2–4).

In John 4 we see Christ engaging a Samaritan woman in conversation—something that shocked his disciples. Not only that, but Jesus had asked for and accepted a drink from her—even handling a drinking vessel used by a Samaritan would have made a Jew unclean, but Jesus is unfazed. He does not deem her strange relational history "clean," but his ability to step over the boundaries and meet her where she is opens up a means by which she can find cleansing.

In Luke 8 we find a woman plagued by hemorrhages creeping up to Jesus and touching the edge of his cloak. Jesus stops and turns. "Who touched me?" he demands. You can imagine her fear—she, not only a woman, but a diseased one at that, had touched him and now he was going to punish her for it. Unable to hide, she comes "trembling" to his feet and tells him what she has done. Again, it is Christ's words that provide part of the healing: he calls her "daughter"—a term he uses nowhere else in the Gospels—and so deems her clean (vv. 43–48).

In Luke 5 we see four friends breaking open the roof of a house and lowering their crippled friend down to Jesus. What is interesting is that Christ first forgives the man's sins and then heals him, saying that the healing is proof of his authority to forgive. In other words he is directly challenging the mechanisms of forgiveness that the Pharisees thought they had exclusive control over. Not only will Jesus challenge the dirt boundaries, but he will challenge the very means of cleansing those who were classified as dirty in the first place.

Just after this, Luke goes on to describe how Jesus dined with Levi and "a large crowd of tax collectors." We have already seen how inviting someone for dinner is a gift that carries with it the potential for relationship—so the fact that Christ was happy to accept such a gift from "sinners," as the watching Pharisees call them, is another example of his willingness to step over dirt boundaries and meet people where they were. We can note from this that, again, he does not deem the tax collectors as "clean," but is clear that he has "not come to call the righteous, but sinners to repentance" and that the means to doing that is not to stand on the other side and exclude them as "dirt" but to eat alongside them (vv. 27–33).

In Luke 7 and 8 we see two examples of Jesus raising the dead, and in both situations Jesus again challenges our perceptions of what is clean and what is dirty. In Luke 7:14 we are told that Jesus "went up and touched the coffin" before commanding the boy to live, and in Luke 8:54 Jesus "took [the girl] by the hand" and restored her to life.

Finally, in Luke 19 we see Jesus driving the "robbers" out of the temple. On the surface it appears that Jesus is actually "cleansing" the temple of this "dirt," but he is not. What he is actually doing is getting rid of those who sought to turn a profit from those who came for cleansing at the temple. He is clearing the way *for* the dirty, giving them free access to the means of forgiveness without having to purchase special money to buy special sacrifices.

These episodes from the Gospels show us three ways in which Christ forces us to reevaluate our dirt boundaries. First, he erases some of them. Certain things that we call dirty, he considers clean. Second, he shows us that even if something is itself "dirty," contact with it does not make us dirty. Even if certain things do remain "dirt," it is up to us to get alongside them and be in relationship with them, to sit down and eat with them and receive their generosity. Third, Christ shows us that the mechanisms of cleansing need to be kept clear, that dirt should be given free access to the temple. Simply excluding what is dirty goes no way toward helping it to be clean.

These reevaluations were too much for the religious leaders of Christ's day. Their well-ordered society could not tolerate this man who stepped freely over dirt boundaries and claimed to come back with clean feet, who tore down other boundaries altogether and then invited those who were dirty to come and be cleaned.[2] He seemed to have no idea about the dangers of infection or the proper means of forgiveness. Here he was, doling it out for free in the streets and undermining their monopoly and tidy profits. He either had to clean up his act or be expelled as dirty.

It is my belief that the church today is in many ways acting like these imperialists, these white supremacists, these Pharisees. We are too eager to label things as dirty and stay in our clean, well-ordered constructs. We not only refuse to get our hands dirty but bar the way for the dirty to find cleansing. I am convinced that, in contrast, the Emergent Church will succeed—not because it liberally calls everything clean, but because it will be open to its environment, happy to cross boundaries and for its boundaries to be crossed. Commenting on the criticism that such people or churches beyond Stage 4 might be

170

seen as just "wishy-washy neutrals," Fowler argues that their "radical openness to the truth of the other stems precisely from their confidence in the reality mediated by their own tradition and in the awareness that reality overspills their mediation."[3] If we are to find the whole truth, we must be confident enough and conjunctive enough to step over that which has been labeled "dirty" or "untouchable," and see that some angle on truth might lie there. As mentioned before, if we are prepared to step outside the "cleanliness" of our churches and into our communities we will be surprised at what riches we find. Indeed, it may even be the case that the cleanliness of the church is preventing us from appreciating truth.

Contemplating his childhood as the son of a Lutheran pastor, the psychologist Carl Jung attached great significance to an experience he had at age twelve. He was admiring the cathedral in his hometown of Basel and recalls it in the collection of his *Memories, Dreams and Reflections*:

> One fine summer day . . . I came out of school at noon and went to the cathedral square. The sky was gloriously blue, the day one of radiant sunshine. The roof of the cathedral glittered, the sun sparkling from the new, brightly glazed tiles. I was overwhelmed by the beauty of the sight, and thought: "The world is beautiful and the church is beautiful, and God made all this and sits above it far away in the blue sky on a golden throne and . . ." Here came a great hole in my thoughts, and a choking sensation. I felt numbed, and knew only: "Don't go thinking now! Something terrible is coming" . . . I gathered all my courage, as though I were about to leap forthwith into hell-fire, and let the thought come. I saw before me the cathedral, the blue sky. God sits on His golden throne, high above the world—and from under the throne an enormous turd falls upon the sparkling new roof, shatters it, and breaks the walls of the cathedral asunder.[4]

Surprisingly to him, he did not feel condemned by the image. Quite the opposite. "I felt an enormous, an indescribable relief. Instead of the expected damnation, grace had come upon me and with it an unutterable bliss such as I had never known." Jung connected this experience with that of his father's church. He felt that the Protestant ideal, with its emphasis on the object, tended to

> fix the ideal—Christ—in its outward aspect and thus rob it of its mysterious relation to the inner man. It is this prejudice which impels the Protestant interpreters of the Bible to interpret . . . the Kingdom of God as being "among you" instead of "within you." . . . Christ the ideal took upon himself the sins of the world. But if the ideal is wholly outside then the sins of the individual are also outside, and consequentially he is more of a fragment than ever, since superficial misunderstanding conveniently enables him, quite literally, to "cast his sins upon Christ" and thus evade his deepest responsibilities—which is contrary to the spirit of Christianity.[5]

By pushing all our sin, or dirt, "outside," we risk abdicating our responsibility to do something about the roots of it and actually do damage to our psyche. Simply pushing it out of the door and trying to forget it happened simply wouldn't do for Jung, and as we have seen, nor would it do for Christ either. If Christ's power lies in being able to cleanse, then a church where no dirt is allowed in is powerless. From his other writings we find out that Jung's father was a minister for whom the church had become lifeless, and Jung viewed him as a reliable but powerless figure in charge of a church "purified to the point of sterility." It was a church that had become inbred, whose gene pool was in desperate need of some enrichment, and Jung's vision was of a God doing this re-fertilization, dramatically putting dirt back in the very place where it could experience cleansing, and thus of a God concerned that the church regain its place and authority as the locus for our essential "dirt work."

For too long the church has been a place that has excluded, rather than included. It has been very happy to set rigid dirt boundaries, but then it has not only been slow to reevaluate the validity of them, but also has often refused either to step over them and show compassion to the "dirty," or to even open its doors to them. Where are the churches courageous enough to protect the pedophiles from the vigilante mobs and help them back to normality? I wonder, if Charles Manson survives to be released from prison, how many churches will welcome him in? I am convinced that Christ would do so without even demanding that he repent first, for the body of Christ is where dirt comes to be cleansed, not where the clean come to take refuge from dirt.

We might initially be surprised that Jung's vision was actually a moment of grace, but in many ways dirt can operate in this transformative way; we have already seen how gifts are often used to mark transitions or rites of passage, but there are situations where dirt functions this way too. Perhaps the most familiar examples come out of our wedding traditions. Bachelor and bachelorette parties provide an opportunity for the bride and groom to be mildly "sullied" by their respective gender communities before being sent off to marriage. The best man will then traditionally in his speech ceremonially dish some dirt about the groom. In doing so the idea is not that the groom is humiliated, but that he is brought closer to us, brought down to earth so that we can connect better with him and thus participate more fully in his transformation from friend to husband.

In this situation, the best man is functioning as a "trickster." Trickster figures appear in virtually all cultures, and stories about them show that their regular function is to play with dirt and mediate a transformation with it. One of the trickster figures in Islam is the mystical poet Rumi, founder of the whirling dervishes. Many of his poems (which have been beautifully translated by Coleman Barks in *The Essential Rumi*) deal with dirt, but I particularly like "Dervish at the Door" because of the way it also links with gift.

Dervish at the Door

A dervish knocked at a house
to ask for a piece of dry bread,
or moist, it didn't matter.
"This is not a bakery," said the owner.
"Might you have a piece of gristle then?"
"Does this look like a butchershop?"
"A little flour?"
"Do you hear a grinding stone?"
"Some water?"
"This is not a well."
Whatever the dervish asked for,
the man made some tired joke
and refused to give him anything.
Finally the dervish ran into the house,
lifted his robe, and squatted
as though to take a shit.

"Hey, hey!"
"Quiet, you sad man. A deserted place
is a fine spot to relieve oneself,
and since there's no living thing here,
or means of living, it needs fertilizing."
The dervish began his own list
of questions and answers.
"What kind of bird are you? Not a falcon,
trained for the royal hand. Not a peacock,
painted with everyone's eyes. Not a parrot,
that talks for sugar cubes. Not a nightingale,

174

Cities / Gift / Dirt

that sings like someone in love.
Not a hoopoe bringing messages to Solomon,
or a stork that builds on a cliffside.
What exactly do you do?
You are no known species.
You haggle and make jokes
to keep what you own for yourself.
You have forgotten the One
who doesn't care about ownership,
who doesn't try to turn a profit
from every human exchange."

Translated by Coleman Barks[6]

We see here again the connection between market economics and spiritual sterility. The dervish identifies the house
as a barren wasteland because everything in it is designed
to turn a profit . . . And so decides it needs some fertilizing with the gift of a bit of dirt. We can therefore see dirt
functioning to bring some life back into a dead situation.
Matter is deliberately put out of place, the normal order
of things is changed, and life sparks back where there was
none. We get hints of this now in the cross-dressing in
pantomimes, and we see similar things happening historically in carnivals. In the Roman Saturnalia carnival, the
roles of slaves and masters were reversed for a day, and
the slaves were served at tables by their masters. During
the Middle Ages the annual Feast of Fools provided some
relief from the harshness of the Catholic Church. One
shocked diarist described such an event he'd seen in the
French provinces:

> In the very midst of divine service masqueraders with gro-
> tesque faces, disguised as women, lions and mummers,
> performed their dances, sang indecent songs in the choir,
> ate their greasy food from a corner of the altar near the
> priest celebrating mass, got out their games of dice, burned

a stinking incense made of old shoe leather, and ran and
hopped about all over the church.[7]

Others have described how excrement was sometimes
burned instead of incense and how sometimes the clergy
were paraded about in carts filled with manure. As Lewis
Hyde puts it, "Mocking but not changing the order of things,
ritual dirt-work operates as a kind of safety-valve, allowing
internal conflicts and nagging anomalies to be expressed
without serious consequence."[8] Even so, carnival was a
space for different worlds to be imagined, for those who
were oppressed to experience the realization that if things
could be different for one day, they could be made different
permanently in time.

One function of tricksters, then, is to throw some dirt
around and put on a carnival—to allow steam to be let
off and new ways to be imagined. In this sense, tricksters
can nudge us from one stage of faith to another. We see
an example of this in Acts 10, where God plays trickster
with Peter and throws some "dirt" around by asking him
to enjoy food designated as unclean. One might see the
result of Peter's exposure to this divine dirt as a movement
from Stage 3—where he referenced an external authority
to decide on the cleanliness of food and people—to Stage 4
or even 5, where his "internal" vision through the Spirit
within him became a new source of authority. The result of
this movement was certainly a more conjunctive outlook:
he was able to accept that "dirty" Gentiles were also free
to be baptized and receive the Spirit.

Occasionally, though, tricksters do more than this and
catalyze moments of radical change. In Alaskan folklore
there is a trickster figure called Raven. In one story about
Raven the world is very thirsty because another character,
Petrel, is hoarding all the water and guarding the spring
where it bubbles up. Raven goes to Petrel's hut and tries to

176

coax Petrel away from the spring by telling him to look at all the amazing things happening outside, but Petrel won't budge. Petrel goes to sleep guarding the spring and the water; Raven sleeps there too. Early in the morning Raven wakes up and sees Petrel sound asleep, so he goes outside, gets some dog-dirt, and spreads it all over Petrel's backside. When Petrel wakes up, Raven cries out to him that he has soiled himself and Petrel runs off to clean up, whereupon Raven takes the lid off the spring and starts drinking. As he flies away, water falls from his beak to the ground, so creating all the rivers and creeks in Alaska.[9]

This is a different kind of trickster story, for in it we see not a time of harmless release but a radical change in the world. There is gift here too: the water and life-giving rivers and creeks come as a gift from heaven, and specifically as the result of a god being degraded. "Dirt brings gift from heaven" is a classic pattern that is repeated in many trickster stories throughout the world. Lewis Hyde concludes from his extensive study of them that, "as a rule, Trickster takes a god who lives on high and debases him or her with earthly dirt—or appears to debase, for in fact the usual consequence of this dirtying is the god's eventual renewal."[10]

In light of this we can see Christ doing "dirt work" in a new way. Not only does he challenge our dirt boundaries, stepping over them, erasing them and clearing the way for us to step back over them, but he acts as trickster too. Christ did what all at Stage 6 are called to do: he subverted our dirt boundaries and paid the price for it. But the wonderful mystery of the Trinity is that Christ simultaneously acted as the trickster playing with dirt and debasing God on high, and the God being debased. And debased is exactly what Christ was, for if dirt is "matter out of place," what could be more out of place, and thus more filthy, than God nailed to a cross, naked and bloody? The Old Testament tells us that anyone hung from a tree is cursed (Deut. 21:23) and

Paul uses this text to argue that on the cross we see Christ "becoming a curse for us" (Gal. 3:13). God became dirt for us, but through this sullying of God with earthly dirt, we in fact see the miracle of God's renewal. A gift from heaven comes to us; the temple curtain is ripped and heaven and earth are brought closer.

It is no sterile church where this invigorating mystery is allowed to be told. Yet we have disinfected it and sanitized it as Rite One communion, pushing the dirt out and so preventing the way for the dirty to come and find cleansing. In doing so we risk Christ turning trickster on us just as he did with the Pharisees, calling them whitewashed tombs that look beautiful on the outside but are actually full of dirt and death. We risk him boldly stepping over the dirt boundaries we have set up and being happy to be found with those we have classified as sinners. Martin Luther King played trickster with the racists, Gandhi played trickster with the imperialists, and Christ played trickster with the temple. And through some organ he will play trickster with the church: turning over tables, threatening to pull it down and rebuild it—and finally ripping the curtain in it from top to bottom . . . All of this will appear to "dirty" it, but all of it will lead to its eventual renewal. God had no place for proud priests who barred people's way into heaven, and he will have no place for a hierarchical, top-down, sterile church that refuses to function as it should as the place for dirt work.

If this is the case, one might ask then what form this trickster-Christ might take now? In the past the church has given space to "dirt rituals." Many historians now agree that the ritual debasing of a papal effigy in an annual carnival played a key role in catalyzing the Reformation in Germany—the same Reformation that ironically then did away with carnivals and feasts in its drive to clean up the church. We still suffer their cleansing now in the paucity of dirt ritual in the church, but tricksters are nonetheless still at work behind the scenes. The subtitle of Hyde's book on tricksters is "Mischief, Myth and Art" and he proposes that art ought to function as the modern-day trickster to our society. Interestingly, one of the artists he cites as performing this function is Andres Serrano, who produced the now notoriously named "Piss Christ" image. This is a photograph of a cheap, kitsch crucifix with a wooden cross and white plastic Jesus shot through a filter of urine. Other shots in the same series are photographed through water tinged with blood or human milk. The exhibition of these images was met with total outrage by the conservative and Christian right in the United States, who were shocked that the National Endowment for the Arts had given Serrano financial support. They saw the works as blasphemous and campaigned successfully to virtually destroy federal support for the arts in the US in the early 1990s. Yet for his own part, Serrano defended his work:

> Complex and unresolved feelings about my own Catholic upbringing inform this work which helps me to redefine and personalize my relationship with God. For me, art is a moral and spiritual obligation that cuts across all manner of pretense and speaks directly to the soul. Although I am no longer a member of the Catholic Church, I consider myself a Christian and I practice my faith through my work.[11]

Serrano was attempting to play trickster: by surrounding the overfamiliar crucifix in "dirty" human fluids he was trying to get us to reimagine the pain and suffering of the cross and thus to work a renewal to "save the divine from its own too-elevated purity" as Hyde puts it. He paid the price for his "dirt work" with his vilification by the Christian right.

Serrano was learning Fowler's clear lesson: playing trickster with a powerful and conservative church is a dangerous business. But play we must if we are to rescue the church from its sterility and make it again a place where people can come and do their "dirt work" without feeling condemned. Our experience at Vaux has been that many of the people we have had coming to services are people who have been made to feel "dirty" or guilty by their churches. It has always been our hope that at Vaux they found a space where they could do their "dirt work" and feel welcomed and accepted as they did it. We have always tried to construct our services so that they facilitated this, and in this sense we—as has much of the alternative worship scene—have functioned as trickster. That has in turn resulted in some notoriety.

Having thrown ideas of dirt around for some time, we decided to do a series of services tackling the issue. The first of these services was "reviewed" by Steve Collins and his report posted on the Christian website, *Ship of Fools*. His review, under the title "How Far Is Too Far?"[12] asked people to reflect on and debate three elements of the service that might have been particularly shocking. He, wisely as it turned out, framed the discussion with the advice that "those who attended found this a powerful and intense act of worship. Those who only read about it may misunderstand and take offence."

The first element he raised was the use of a slide as people entered the building that said "God is found in the shit." It was used after a lot of very intense and careful debate in the group, who decided that its clearly shocking language actually forced us to accept the difficult and profound truth that God really does never leave us, in a way that more polite forms simply could not. As Collins explained, "We struggle with the propriety of putting God and shit in the same sentence. Yet the Incarnation brought them into closer contact than that." If God can be found here, then we have grounds for a genuine hope, regardless of our background and situation, regardless of what we have done, and sometimes it takes the dragging of language that is freely in use "on the street" into the "clean" context of church for us to let this truth really get beyond the carefully compartmentalized "holy bits" of us.

The second element of the service under discussion was a meditation based on Serrano's "Piss Christ" image discussed above, to which I will add no more. The third was the communion. Collins describes it well:

> The altar is a small white cube. [N] stands behind it, loaf in hand, explaining what this ritual means. He speaks calmly, so we are unprepared for what is coming. This is Christ's body, broken for you. And he throws the bread down on the floor. This is Christ's blood, shed for you. And he throws the wine across the altar. It runs onto the floor like blood. We sit there, stunned. This is more shocking than anything before. Unexpected, ungentle, truthful. M picks up the bread and puts the pieces on the altar. She pours out more glasses of wine, but does not pick up the one spilled. We come up two by two. On each side of the altar is a mirror; as we kneel we watch ourselves receive and on it is written "You are my body."

As Collins said, it was a powerful and intense act of worship. But it was also extremely heartfelt and in no way designed as a gimmick. What was clear from talking to people afterward was that they had genuinely been able to engage in the communion in a way that they had not before, that the whole service had allowed them to do "dirt work" in a supportive and caring environment.

After the report was published the chat rooms on the website were opened and people invited to comment, which they did in droves. Ironically, none of the contributors had been at the service, but many were freely making up details about it to support their various arguments. We were, among other things, accused of having performed a "black mass" and of being faithless backsliders just out to shock. The truth quickly disappeared into myth, and various legends about exactly what happened began to gain credence—the virtual reality became stronger than reality itself. It seemed that our attempt to play trickster had met much the same problem as Serrano's: the public perception and hype had taken over from the personally and communally successful reinvigoration of a purified Christ.

I mention this as a warning. If I am right that the Emergent Church is going to have to be a place where dirt boundaries are reassessed, then it is likely that it will face pressure and attention, because what it will do will likely be seen as shocking; the conjunctive viewpoint often is, to the Stage 3 observer. This must not deter the church from its task. None of us are without dirt, and all of us need places to deal with it. The church ought to be the place where that can happen, because we believe that in his divine trickster role Christ has done something unique. But with it currently "purified to the point of sterility," people are ignoring the church as a place of "dirt work" and turning to therapists, Jerry Springer, and chat rooms. Not that these should be necessarily knocked—on the contrary, I wish more Christians would realize their need to go beyond a weekly prayer-dousing and actually use a therapist to do proper "dirt work" in a professional context—but like the gift, unless the dirt goes out of sight at some point—can be offered to the divine truly to deal with it—then it is in danger of cycling round and round and round and dragging us down.

As the body of Christ we are called to do as Christ did: to erase the dirt boundaries that the powerful religious have constructed, to step over those boundaries that remain and be incarnate wherever there is dirt, and to turn over the tables, rip the curtains, and clear the way for the dirty to enter the temple and find cleansing. Philip Larkin described the church as "a serious house, on serious earth";[13] I believe that Christ would criticize us for overseriousness, encourage us to lighten up and allow some muddy hands to grasp again our sterilized liturgies. To achieve this we will require tricksters to have courage, jump up with cheeky smiles, write their lyrics, do their art, play their music, and turn their tricks. As Ezra Pound said, "Humanity is the rich effluvium; it is the waste and the manure and the soil and from it grows the tree of the arts."[14] Wherever they are, in alternative worship, in youth groups, in the dark, awkward, Stage 4 corners of our Stage 3 congregations, the tricksters must be coaxed out to help us find our dirt and nourish this tree, for our survival depends on them. They may not be easy to find, but one can be fairly sure that they will not be decked in white, waiting around.

Conclusion.

The Emergence
of Christ

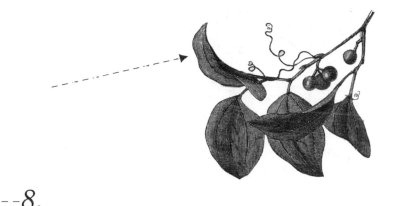

------8.

{ The Emergence of Christ }

I began this book by proposing that the church had reached a local maximum, and that in order to survive, it needs to progress and find a new way of being in an evolving world. Using Fowler's stages of faith, I have argued that the church needs to descend from its pre-Enlightenment Stage 3 naïveté into the valleys of unknowing, where it must be reincarnated, as Christ was, into specific places and cultures. Only then can it begin to move into the Stage 5 conjunctivity of a post-Enlightenment incarnation, where it can hold together those at other points of the journey of faith without abuses of power or destructive infighting. In Christ we, the body of Christ, have a wonderful model of how this change might be effected, and, as many other institutions seek to make similar changes to their structures and outlooks, we have a unique opportunity to witness to them and help them change too.

I have also proposed that there are two ways that we could go about this journey, two possible modes of change: revolution or evolution. Revolution is characterized by speed and violence. It is about divide and rule. It tries to impose change from without. It is top down and heavily dependent on hierarchies and centralized power. Evolution refuses to rush ahead and thus avoids shearing and fissures. It tries to bring about change from within. It is about empowerment. It is bottom up and dependent on distributed knowledge.

In Christ's coming to earth, we see God finally critiquing revolution as ineffective. The top-down system of the law, the temple, and the priests—all of which Paul tells us end up condemning us without changing us—are superseded in this new covenant, which promises to change us from within. In Christ, we see God modeling a bottom-up emergent system that can transform us in this new way, and calling us onto this path of spiritual evolution as we seek higher places.

Yet before this change can occur, we have seen in Christ's advent that we must stop and wait, and thus allow the old order of things to die. We must grieve this loss and accept fully that it has gone, for only true grief will provide us with the empty hands we will need to accept the new. We must then admit that God has the holy freedom to do as God pleases, for only once we have gotten beyond co-opting God into our programs will we have ground to hope that genuine newness will come. Finally, as we wait, we must exercise our memories, for it is the only way that we can escape the absolute present and know that the future can be different.

In Christ's incarnation we have seen that real, transformative change starts very small. It is not explosive. There is no "shock and awe," only quiet amazement from outcast shepherds and stargazing astrologers at "how silently, how silently, the wondrous gift is given." Its significance is missed by the religious, and the powerful see it as a threat, but it lies embedded nonetheless—slowly, slowly growing. We must become these wombs of the divine if we are to see the church reborn.

In Christ's emerging we have seen that he deliberately set out to model a new way, one that refused to buy devotion or stun people into it. It was a ministry based on gift; a ministry that radically reevaluated dirt boundaries; a ministry that held true to these principles through success and condemnation, hatred and death.

In Christ's approach to the city, we can model God's emerging vision for our future as urban, precisely because, even though many of us do not live in cities, the city reaches out and touches us wherever we do live, and the city is the place where we most clearly see divinity and all the diversity of humanity cooperating and cohabiting. In an urbanizing world, I do not think it is overstepping the mark to say that the future of the church is tied up in its ability to function and succeed in the city space.

Moreover, our communities and cities themselves are complex, emergent structures, so we see this virtuous circle emerging:

- God in Christ has moved from a hierarchical, top-down approach to an emergent, bottom-up one;
- God sees the city—the coming New Jerusalem—as the perfect symbol of divine and human cooperation;
- the city is a complex, emergent structure.

It would appear then that the church, as a complex, emergent organization, working in the city, is the natural integration of the way of the city and the way of Christ. The science of complexity offers us some key truths about what sort of organisms will become self-renewing and self-organizing: those that are mildly regulated, steered away from the death of rigidity or anarchy, and held in the place of life at the "edge of chaos." And our rational science is backed up by God's metaphysical truths: that the body of Christ will become an organ of transformation for people only when it functions in an incarnational, conjunctive, and emergent way.

Christ's life, the life of our communities, and the growing science of complexity come together with unique synergy to provide spiritual, social, and rational imperatives for the church to become an emergent system. However, we are the body of Christ only because of Christ's death and resurrection, and we have seen that it was part of the very character of Cain's original city project that spurred his descendants on to take up weapons again, expel Christ from the city, and kill him outside its walls.

Before we can settle on emergence as the way forward, then, we must not just be satisfied that it is supported in the life of Christ and the city, but in Christ's death at the hands of the city, and his subsequent resurrection in it too. I am convinced that in Christ's death we see him not just becoming gift, and so offering the final criticism of a world that would like to pay for salvation and be done with the relationships; not just becoming dirt and playing trickster, and so offering the final criticism of a world that seeks to put up boundaries, exclude people, and bar the way to cleansing; but re-emerging, and so offering the final criticism of a world that seeks to control God, co-opt God, put God in a box, and relate to God on its own terms. In order to explore this proposition, I want to look in particular at the events surrounding Judas's betrayal of Christ, and Christ's subsequent death and resurrection.

John 13:18–30 tells us:

"I am not referring to all of you; I know those I have chosen. But this is to fulfil the scripture: 'He who shares my bread has lifted up his heel against me.'

"I am telling you now before it happens, so that when it does happen you will believe that I am He. I tell you the truth, whoever accepts anyone I send accepts me; and whoever accepts me accepts the one who sent me."

After he had said this, Jesus was troubled in spirit and testified, "I tell you the truth, one of you is going to betray me."

His disciples stared at one another, at a loss to know which of them he meant. One of them, the disciple whom Jesus loved, was reclining next to him. Simon Peter motioned to this disciple and said, "Ask him which one he means."

Leaning back against Jesus, he asked him, "Lord, who is it?"

Jesus answered, "It is the one to whom I will give this piece of bread when I have dipped it in the dish." Then, dipping the piece of bread, he gave it to Judas Iscariot, son of Simon. As soon as Judas took the bread, Satan entered into him.

"What you are about to do, do quickly," Jesus told him, but no one at the meal understood why Jesus said this to him. Since Judas had charge of the money, some thought Jesus was telling him to buy what was needed for the Feast, or to give something to the poor. As soon as Judas had taken the bread, he went out. And it was night.

Judas Iscariot is in many ways Christ's shadow. Where Christ was happy to give and receive gifts, Judas the accountant worried about wasting money. Where Christ was happy to step over dirt boundaries, Judas the zealot was concerned with reinforcing them. And as Christ approached his death and life from the bottom up, working an evolutionary change from within, Judas approached his death from the top down, trying to spark off a revolution.

However, the question remains: why did Judas decide to betray Jesus at this *particular* time? What was it about what happened in that last supper that finally catalyzed him into action and sent him out into the night?

Jesus senses Judas's dark thoughts of betrayal immediately after he has told the disciples that "whoever accepts anyone I send accepts me; and whoever accepts me accepts the one who sent me." I would like to propose that Judas was perhaps the only one among the disciples who actually understood the significance of these words.

Judas was certainly no "dumb betrayer." It is thought that he was the only one of the Twelve who was from Judea rather than Galilee, the northern region that was very much sneered at by those in power in the south in Jerusalem. In John 7:52 we find the Pharisees belittling Nicodemus as he pleaded for sense by saying, "Are you from Galilee, too? Look into it, and you will find that a prophet does not come out of Galilee." This reflects the attitude we see in John 1:46 where Nathanael mocks the Galilean town of Nazareth, scoffing, "Can anything good come from there?" It is likely that Judas thought himself superior to these country boys; that he knew better. He was certainly the only disciple described as having a specific responsibility in the group as its accountant, and though it is pure speculation to say that he might have been the best educated, one might surmise that he would at least have considered himself different.

In any event, Judas appears to find these words of Jesus particularly troubling. Perhaps he is disappointed that after Jesus's triumphal entry into Jerusalem he has not gone ahead and made his power play, starting the revolution to overthrow the Roman occupation and establish a Jewish state. Instead of acting like an overlord, Jesus has started the Passover meal by acting like a servant and gone around washing everyone's feet. Not only that, but when he says,

"Whoever accepts anyone I send accepts me; and whoever accepts me accepts the one who sent me," he appears in these words to be questioning the validity of the whole temple system and its hierarchy. If Jesus can distribute his authority to anybody, and anyone who accepts Jesus through them accepts God, then what is the point of the priests and the sacrifices and the whole Jewish construct?

Judas would have known that Jesus had talked about pulling the temple down and rebuilding it in three days, but this went beyond even that. Jesus seemed to be proposing that access to God would be a free-for-all for anyone who accepted Christ from any of his believers. This attitude would have challenged everything Judas had stood for and believed in. Although not designated a "Zealot" as Simon was, Judas seems to come across as very hard line, a "loyalist Stage 3" perhaps, and, like many of Jesus's other followers, was probably expecting Jesus to take on a political role. John 6:15 tells us they had intended to "come and make him king by force" before—perhaps by forcing the situation now, Judas could catalyze Jesus into action before he followed through this crackpot idea of free access to God.

In betraying Jesus then, perhaps Judas is not so much doing so out of hate, out of a desire to see him dead, but out of frustration that Jesus was not playing the role everyone was expecting him to. The rest of the country boys could sit around and wait; Judas was going to engage in some direct action: contrive a confrontation between Jesus, the religious leaders, and the Romans and so force Jesus's hand, compelling him to act.

Luke 22 tells us that "the chief priests . . . were looking for some way to get rid of Jesus. . . . And Judas went to [them to discuss] with them how he might betray Jesus" (vv. 2, 4). The other Gospel writers concur, adding that for a sum of money Judas agreed to find some way to "hand

Jesus over to them." We are told that the chief priests were worried about arresting Jesus during the feast, for fear that the people would riot, and it seems very unlikely that they would not have communicated their worries to the very person who was going to do the deed. Perhaps Judas was guilty of naïveté, thinking he could bluff the priests, timing his betrayal precisely when they didn't want it, simultaneously creating a popular uprising and giving Jesus a window of political opportunity to start his revolution. Excited by his plan, he joins the others in the upper room, waiting for the right moment to precipitate Jesus's move to glorious victory. . . .

Yet talk at the meal turns to betrayal, and when Judas is handed the fateful piece of bread by Jesus, Matthew records him as protesting, "Surely not I, Rabbi?" In this we see Judas objecting to the thought that what he is about to do is really a betrayal. It is certainly interesting that it is at this precise moment when Jesus breaks bread with Judas that all the Gospel writers pinpoint his decision to "betray" him. Surely there would have been better times? What was it about these words of Jesus and the act of being handed a piece of broken bread that sent him into action? The symbolism of the broken bread and shared wine (which Luke suggests Judas was still present to see) seems to consolidate Judas's fears about Jesus's course of action. Again, I want to suggest that perhaps Judas was the only one to understand its significance: if Christ's body was shared among them, then his power and authority was shared too. If Christ's life-blood was drunk by all of them, then Christ's life was no longer located in one person and in one place. This invalidated the whole concept of the temple-state and need for the Jews' self-rule, and thus ran right up against the political ambitions and dreams that many assume Judas to have had.

Perhaps Judas thought that as Jesus was still just talking symbolically about a "time that is coming" he still had time to divert him to another course of action: he has to go to the priests now, before it is too late. He gets up and leaves, stepping into the dark night. He knows Jesus and the rest of them will more than likely head out to the Mount of Olives after supper, so he tells the priests to gather a guard and go and seize him there. It must have taken some time, for Jesus spent this time praying in anguish about what was coming. The priests were probably enjoying their feasting too and needed persuading that, given the tinderbox situation with the people, now was the best time to act.

Eventually they must have agreed; they summoned some temple guards and some Roman soldiers for good measure and went out to capture him. Luke tells us that "a crowd" was with them. Judas led the way. Perhaps he was bubbling over with excitement at everything coming together so well: the following crowd would be ready to riot as soon as Jesus was taken, and Jesus would then surely start the revolution. So, probably still thinking that he had done the right thing and that Jesus would actually be pleased with his cunning plan, he strode up to Jesus and kissed him. Things certainly started well—some swords were drawn and a fight broke out. One of the chief priest's servants went down with a blow to the head. . . .

But then disaster struck. Jesus commanded them to stop fighting. He went to the servant and healed him. He asked them, "Am I leading a rebellion, that you have come out with swords and clubs?" "Yes! Yes, you are!" we can imagine Judas crying in desperation as the realization dawned on him that Jesus wasn't. Jesus was led away. He didn't intend to fight. The country boys scattered in fear. Judas had failed. He had betrayed an innocent man. Seeing that he had sent Jesus to his death, racked with grief and "seized with remorse," Judas threw the money back in the priests' faces, went to a field, and took his own life.

We are often encouraged to meditate on characters from Scripture and read their stories into ours. We reflect on the part of ourselves that is Peter, denying Christ but later restored. Or Martha, working so hard by ourselves when we should be carefree like Mary. But to look into ourselves and try to see Judas is off-limits. Judas is never redeemed. Judas is dirt, and dirt is to be excluded, pushed away, hidden. Yet what Jung and Christ seem to agree on is that rather than push our dirt into hidden corners, we must bring it into the open, from the subconscious to the conscious, from the dark places to the altar, where it can be properly dealt with.

It is far safer to label Judas as filth, seal him away as the betrayer, and forget about him. But if we do so we are being a closed system, refusing to make that vital feedback connection, and learn from past mistakes. Judas is not to be venerated, but surely his remorse and grief should be respected as heartfelt. We certainly have no reason to believe they were not genuine, and in fact we see the apostles themselves perhaps being more forgiving than we have been. In Acts 1, Judas is described simply as the "guide for those who arrested Jesus." Their admission that he was "one of our number and shared in this ministry" and their subsequent decision to find one to replace him perhaps suggest that they were able to acknowledge that his failed plan was something that they had all thought of at some time.

I believe that we exclude Judas and his dirt from our meditations at our peril. We need to acknowledge, as the apostles perhaps did, that there is a part of Judas in each of us. For we are all Judas when we try to co-opt Christ into our own agenda. We are all Judas when we try to force Christ's hand. We are all Judas when we try to box Christ up for ourselves and control other people's access to him. We are all Judas when we pretend that Christ is located in

196

one place or one person and that all who come to God must come in a particular way in a particular style. And we are all Judas when we try to compel Christ into revolution.

If I am right about Judas, then he was the only one of Jesus's followers actually to understand the significance of his breaking bread, and the power of this realization panicked him into betrayal. One might even speculate that "Satan entered him" because in horror the devil saw Judas's understanding and had to eliminate it. But it was too late. It was as if Judas saw in Christ a nuclear explosion about to go off, and not realizing that this was precisely what Christ's destiny was, he tried to make Christ safe and controllable, but inadvertently sparked off the chain reaction that saw his body obliterated in a megaton fission.

No power on earth was ever going to fix Christ in one place anymore. On the cross we see the beginning of the final act of God's decentralization. God is no longer going to be held captive in the temple, bound by rules, God's people prevented from gaining access by trench lines of priests, money changers, and market sellers. The curtain is ripped. God has exploded. The vial has smashed and the virus has escaped. The emergent Christ has been unleashed.

It is only at Pentecost that the rest of the disciples see what Judas might have understood back then. This Jesus, whom they had seen in the flesh and lived with for years, was now here in one place at one time, and mysteriously in another place too. He had transcended the limitations of the physical, and now his Spirit entering them was fulfilling what he had said that fateful night at the Last Supper, what had appeared to scare Judas so much: we all have access to God through him by the Spirit.

This then is Christ emerging: it is Christ disestablishing the need for the temple, for people to gain access to God only by being in one place and through hierarchies of priests; it is Christ establishing his body as a decentralized network

197

of believers, and thus giving birth to a complex, emergent church that could not be destroyed any more easily than the Internet could be. It is, to rephrase St. Augustine, the body of Christ truly becoming the network whose nodes are everywhere and circumference nowhere.

This model of a complex, conjunctive church comes to us from the cities we live in, from the Scriptures we read and the scientists we respect. Socially, economically, scientifically, politically, and spiritually, we are being given a clear message from Christ about the way to turn the church into an organism fit for the challenges of this new century: we must die and re-emerge as the complex body of Christ.

This is nothing new. Though we have often blinded ourselves to it, Christ becoming complex is what we celebrate in the Eucharist. It is a meal to which we are invited, a gift that hangs heavy with potential for relationship in every plane. The bread and wine that begins centralized, in one place, is unleashed as it enters each one gathered and is taken out into the community. We symbolically split Christ up and each take Christ out with us. Thus decentralized, Christ becomes uncontrollable. The gifts of his body and blood have disappeared into mystery, become inseparable from our own flesh, and are spread out with us into our communities in a manner that no power can reverse.

In a world of SARS, AIDS, biological terror threats, and computer viruses, it is the micro, not the macro, that wields power; in the age of infection, simple bandages will not do. It is awe-inspiring to think that 2,000 years ago, before the computer scientists, before the biologists, before the economists, before the sociologists had even invented the language to talk about it, God knew this and acted, putting an end to the top-down system of the temple and disappearing into the viral form of the Spirit.

Unfortunately, we have not been faithful to this vision. We have, like Judas, panicked at the awesome freedom of it, the outrageous grace of it, the unbelievable generosity of it, and decided it will not do. We have, like Judas, tried to co-opt God and talk God out of it. We have created structures and thrown up stone buildings to try to tie God down. We have given ourselves over to priests and told them to represent us before God. We have denied freedom and power to those still heavily infected by God's virus, quarantined them and warned others away.

But God in God's grace will not give up. "There is now no condemnation for those whom Christ has infected." Put simply, the symptoms of the virus that God poured out on the morning of Pentecost were this: that those infected spoke about God in a language people could understand. And over the centuries, God has continued to battle to allow people to speak about and practice their faith in their vernacular. They decided Gentile believers would have to follow Jewish customs; they translated the Scriptures into Latin so that only the educated could read them; they narrowed church music to organs and hymns; they dressed up leaders in strange costumes . . . But each time the virus would not be bottled. The Gentiles were allowed to express their faith without following Mosaic law and being circumcised; the Bible was translated into modern English; the music of the streets is once again beginning to be used in worship.

But there is a long way to go. The church is still obsessed with hierarchy and authority. It is still consumed by sex; still fighting to build up dirt boundaries rather than widening the access for the dirty to be cleansed. It is still clearly recognizable in the sinister caricatures of Philip Pullman's *His Dark Materials* trilogy. In these extraordinary children's books, he describes the church as an institution that oppresses, that is looking to separate people from their souls and is out to hide the truth about the universe. His hero, the scrawny little girl Lyra, battles against these dark forces with a coalition of angels, witches, bears, and other creatures—all fighting for freedom from the "experimental theologians" who are endangering all beings with their crazy devotion to the institution that worships an old and feeble God and seeks a distant kingdom of heaven. The trilogy ends with Lyra meditating that after many battles, now they had rid the world of God, they must "study and work hard, all of us, in all our different worlds, and then we'll build . . . the republic of heaven."[1] It is challenging stuff indeed, and we would be very foolish to ignore his words and the wide impact they are likely to have on a new generation's perception of the church.

We have been given an extraordinary holy freedom. But perhaps Pullman is actually right—in this age of the church we must build the "republic of heaven," because it is only in such a republic that we can hope to avoid the power abuses and dictatorships of the puppet-kings that we inevitably install in God's place.

So, whatever state our churches are in now, we still have this amazing hope: Christ's birth, life, death, and resurrection provide us with an archetype for change and grounds for belief that God is not done yet. It will take time and courage, but we must stop, wait, and grieve. We must let go of our simplistic, mechanistic, legalistic, top-down ideas about God. We must allow God God's holy freedom, and mine the past for hope that the present is not all there is. We must become wombs of the divine and give birth to newness. Slowly, quietly, under the radar of the authorities, we must bring the church down from its local peak to rebirth and nurture it, allowing it to learn from and be dependent on its particular host culture. We must free it to evolve into conjunctivity, rich and complex, networked and decentralized, not allowing it to be co-opted, and always keeping it open to its environment, sensing it, learning from it, responding to it.

In a world of market economics, we must resist the temptation to trade and allow this church to work through the cycle of gift. In a world of exclusion, we must resist the temptation to erect dirt boundaries, but allow it to be trickster and bring renewal through "dirt work." And in the city of Cain, built as a statement of independence against God, we must allow it to be infectious, to shine as a beacon of our destiny: living together as one with God in the city with no temple. Then the church can truly sing its song of ascents. Then the republic can finally return its King.

London, 2006–2007

{ Postscript }

This is a short book by an amateur. While it has sought to discuss issues of conjunctivity, being written from one person's viewpoint it can never itself achieve this state in a satisfactory way; I am keenly aware that what I have written does not contain all the answers.

In order to turn these single-dimension thoughts into something more solid, I wanted to create a space where people could contribute their own perspectives. Perhaps you have stories to tell, or have experience of other denominations or backgrounds. Perhaps you fundamentally disagree with my thesis, or have some slant to add. Either way, it would be great to hear from you; for people on the streets of faith to contribute to a networked discussion of these ideas and see what emerges; to throw some dirt around and exchange some gifts. . . .

Please visit http://kester.typepad.com/signs to join in the conversation.

I look forward to hearing from you.

Peace.

{ Notes }

Introduction

1. R. Descartes, *A Discourse on Method etc.*, first published 1637, part IV.

2. M. Riddell, *Threshold of the Future* (London: SPCK, 1998), 1.

3. G. Cray, ed., *Mission-Shaped Church: Church Planting and Fresh Expressions of Church in a Changing Context* (London: Church House Publishing, 2004), 41.

4. R. S. Thomas, from the collection of poems, *Laboratories of the Spirit* (London: Macmillan, 1975). Used with permission.

5. Quoted in S. R. Covey et al., *First Things First* (London: Simon & Schuster, 1994), 43.

6. J. Fowler, *Stages of Faith: The Psychology of Human Development and the Quest for Meaning* (New York: HarperCollins, 1995), 172.

7. A. Jamieson, *A Churchless Faith: Faith Journeys beyond the Churches* (London: SPCK, 2002), 114. I am perhaps stepping beyond my bounds, but in my work teaching in an inner-city comprehensive school, I have seen many, many examples of students from strongly Stage 3 Pentecostal churches who, in their latter years at school, develop real problems with discipline. I wonder if this is because they have so few role models at the latter stages of faith, and once they begin to appreciate the complexities of their situation in the city have few resources for helping them cope with it, and so end up kicking hard against the system. It is for others to comment in a

more informed way on these casual observations, but perhaps the absence of any Stage 4+ expressions of faith in Pentecostalism is doing young people in troubled communities a great disservice.

8. G. K. Chesterton, *Orthodoxy* (London: House of Stratus, 2001), 58.

9. Quoted in Jamieson, *A Churchless Faith*, 118.

10. Quoted in Fowler, *Stages of Faith*, 200–201.

11. J. Fowler, *Faithful Change: The Personal and Public Challenges of Postmodern Life* (Nashville: Abingdon Press, 1996), 161.

12. Ibid., 166.

13. Ibid., 167.

14. Ibid., 177, italics in original.

15. It is not just Fowler's stages that are transferable from the personal to the institutional. Tools such as the "Enneagram" can also be seen to have relevance for whole churches, rather than just individual people. Reflecting on the nine different types within the Enneagram, it seems that too many "Ones" have been left in charge of the church. Indeed, it seems that many churches are institutionally "One." As Richard Rohr notes, "Ones are inclined to understand themselves as white knights who set forth into the world to save it. [They] carry around a list of other people's mistakes and are resentful of them. Ones are apt to be moral prigs, for ever speaking with upraised index finger and criticising everyone. They can strike people as very arrogant and self-righteous." If we are to be a balanced body, it is vital that we work on not only making sure that our leaderships have a good mix of types, but also that corporately we learn how to mature within each type. With hints of Fowler's "conjunctivity," Rohr continues, "Ones have to learn that there isn't just one right way. . . . Among the lifetime tasks of Ones is to learn occasionally to ignore duty, order and the improvement of the world, and instead to play, celebrate and enjoy life." See R. Rohr and A. Ebert, *The Enneagram: A Christian Perspective*, trans. P. Heinegg (New York: Crossroad Publishing, 2002), 55ff.

16. Ken Loach, "Why did I march? To give the politicians who failed me a lesson in real democracy," *Independent on Sunday*, 23 November 2003, http://news.independent.co.uk/uk/this_britain/article79674.ece.

Chapter 1 Advent

1. G. Cray, ed., *Mission-Shaped Church: Church Planting and Fresh Expressions of Church in a Changing Context* (London: Church House Publishing, 2004), 33–34.

2. From Rowan Williams's foreword to Cray, *Mission-Shaped Church*, vii.

3. A. Kaplan, *Development Practitioners and Social Process: Artists of the Invisible* (London: Pluto Press, 2002), 178.

4. Mao Zedong, quoted in R. Andrews, ed., *The New Penguin Dictionary of Modern Quotations* (London: Penguin, 2001), 285.

5. P. Virilio, *Speed and Politics*, trans. M. Pollizotti (New York: Semiotexte, 1986), 22.

6. Sometimes revolutions do occur where the whole body does experience transformation, but they almost exclusively do so as a response to external factors. To use the disaster on September 11, 2001, in New York as an example, it precipitated a transformation in the practice of many of the organizations affected, but these changes were responses in the face of a catastrophe where a whole body was shaken to its core and a whole body response was required. In this sense, their practice may have been transformed at revolutionary speed, but this violent upheaval was a necessary reflex from within; the same changes could not have been effected by diktat in a more peaceful context without shearing the surface of the body from its core below.

7. A. Toffler, *Future Shock* (London: Pan, 1970), 13.

8. R. Warren, "Towards a Theology of Change," private paper quoted in Cray, *Mission-Shaped Church*, 105.

9. VX01. An extensive archive of Vaux liturgies and writings is available at www.vaux.net.

10. W. Brueggemann, *Hopeful Imagination* (London: SCM Press, 1992), 1, italics in original.

11. Ibid., 6.

12. Cray, *Mission-Shaped Church*, 41.

13. For the sake of clarity, I have borrowed Brueggemann's original headings.

14. The quotes used as subheads in this chapter ("Only grief permits newness," "Only holiness brings hope," and "Only memory allows possibility") are taken from Brueggemann, *Hopeful Imagination*, 4, 49, 89.

15. Cray, *Mission-Shaped Church*, 13.

Chapter 2 Incarnation

1. Adapted from VX12. See www.vaux.net for an extensive archive of Vaux writing.

2. I am speaking metaphorically of course; many see the Apocrypha as one such intertestamental revelation.

3. From VX35.

4. R. Williams, *Writing in the Dust* (London: Hodder & Stoughton, 2002), 80.

5. From VX22.

Chapter 3 Emergence

1. Quoted in J. Jacobs, *The Death and Life of Great American Cities* (New York: Random House, 1961), 433.

2. See S. Johnson, *Emergence: The Connected Lives of Ants, Brains, Cities and Software* (London: Penguin, 2001), 73–99. The parallels this has with our car-filled cities hardly need making. If people never walk through a community, only drive through it, they cannot participate in the low-level interactions that are necessary for emergence. Walking-pace, pavement life means large numbers of eyes and ears looking out for each other, and journeys in cars prevent these essential interactions. As Johnson notes on p. 94, "[Pavements] are the primary conduit for the flow of information between city residents. [They] allow relatively high band-width communication between total strangers . . . they permit local interactions to create global order." See chapters on "The Uses of Sidewalks" and "Erosion of Cities or Attrition of Automobiles," in Jacobs, *Death and Life*.

3. Jacobs, *Death and Life*, 434.

4. As even the most hard-core of Darwinists Richard Dawkins admitted recently on Radio 4, "We alone can rebel against our selfish replicators."

5. R. Sennett, *Flesh and Stone: The Body and the City in Western Civilisation* (London: Norton, 1994), 323.

6. Jacobs, *Death and Life*, 440.

7. "If the doors of perception were cleansed everything would appear to man as it is, infinite." William Blake in *The Marriage of Heaven and Hell*.

8. "You find what you came to find when you're on acid and we've got to start doing it without acid; there's no use opening the door and going through it and then always coming back out again. We've got to move onto the next step." Kesey speaking in Tom Wolfe, *The Electric Kool-Aid Acid Test* (London: Black Swan,1989), 321.

9. Originally published in R. S. Thomas, *Frequencies* (London: Macmillan, 1978). Used with permission.

10. G. Cray, ed., *Mission-Shaped Church: Church Planting and Fresh Expressions of Church in a Changing Context* (London: Church House Publishing, 2004), 77–78.

11. Quoted from their review of Johnson, *Emergence*. David Pogue, "The Swarm," *New York Times*, September 9, 2001.

12. Originally published in Thomas, *Laboratories of the Spirit*, 3. Used with permission.

Chapter 4 The Character of the Emergent Church

1. G. Cray, ed., *Mission-Shaped Church: Church Planting and Fresh Expressions of Church in a Changing Context* (London: Church House Publishing, 2004), ch. 4.

2. Many people have similarly proposed that "cell churches" are emergent. While this is certainly possible, I would argue that in fact most of those I have seen have tended to act more like pyramid schemes, or "clone churches," rather than allowing the genuine, bottom-up freedom that emergence would suggest. In this sense, they seem to be still at Stage 3 and not at the Conjunctive Stage 5 where the Emergent Church needs to be. That said, there appears to be much about the structure of cell churches that could promote emergence.

3. "Conversations: Will Self," *Idler* 2 (November 1993), www.idler .co.uk/archives/will-self/#more-2, accessed January 30, 2007.

4. Cray, *Mission-Shaped Church*, 45.

5. I am indebted to Steven Johnson's excellent account of the development of the scientific thinking surrounding the slime mold in his book *Emergence: The Connected Lives of Ants, Brains, Cities and Software* (London: Penguin, 2001), 11–17.

6. K. Morrison, *School Leadership and Complexity Theory* (London: Routledge, 2002), 15.

7. A Far Side–style example of this dynamic two-way change has been shown in research into the relationship between frogs and flies: frogs develop stickier tongues, while flies develop more slippery feet.

8. J. Donne, "Meditation XVII," *Devotions upon Emergent Occasions* (n.p.: Kessinger Publishing, 2004; orig. pub. 1624), 62.

9. Morrison, *School Leadership*, 15.

10. See chapter 7, "Dirt," for a discussion on why that may not be a bad thing anyway.

11. By this I do not necessarily mean financial dependence. In some areas the church is one of the few institutions actually bringing funds in, and in such cases this essential support must continue. However, decisions on how these funds are used ought to be transparent and perhaps involve local people from outside the core church community.

12. M. de Landa, *A Thousand Years of Nonlinear History* (New York: Zone, 1997), 16.

13. J. Jacobs, *The Death and Life of Great American Cities* (New York: Random House, 1961), 440.

14. M. McMaster, *The Intelligence Advantage: Organizing for Complexity* (Oxford: Butterworth-Heinemann, 1996), xvi.

15. Ibid., 4.

16. Before you ask, yes, these wonderful robots are commercially available at a reasonable price. They're called "thermostatic valves."

17. *"Scientia est Potentia"* is the slogan used by the US government's former "Information Awareness Office," which was run by the former National Security adviser embroiled in the Iran-Contra affair, John Poindexter. The IAO planned a gargantuan database of information about everyone and everything gleaned from digital-trawls through every computer they could get access to. The aim: to use it to track terrorism. The information was not to be shared, leaving us to reflect on Isaac Asimov's warning that "every system of information is dangerous in the extreme. Even if it is used for something trivial, it can subsequently be used for a matter of vital importance." Several of the agency's projects have lived on. See http://nationaljournal.com/about/njweekly/stories/2006/0223nj1.htm for more details.

18. J. Fowler, *Stages of Faith: The Psychology of Human Development and the Quest for Meaning* (New York: HarperCollins, 1995), 186–87.

19. See www.slashdot.org. Again, the full story of the development of Slashdot has been excellently documented by Steven Johnson in *Emergence*, 152ff.

20. Fowler, *Stages of Faith*, 185.

21. See chapter 7, "Dirt," for a wider discussion of the importance of this.

22. A. Huxley, *Ends and Means* (London: Chatto & Windus, 1937), ch. 8.

23. Morrison, *School Leadership*, 22.

Chapter 5 Cities

1. http://www.archis.org/plain/object.php?object=10&year=&num.

2. In actual fact, many believe it was only the protection of the topsoil that allowed cities to develop at all. As Manuel de Landa writes, "Urban life began in Egypt and Mesopotamia precisely because the land was flat and hence not subject to erosion and soil loss." *A Thousand Years of Nonlinear History* (New York: Zone, 1997), 122.

3. M. Fox, *Creation Spirituality* (San Francisco: HarperSanFrancisco, 1991), 7.

4 De Landa, *A Thousand Years*, 26.

5. A. de Botton, *The Art of Travel* (London: Penguin, 2003), 166, 169.

6. Ibid., 178.

7. W. Wordsworth, *The Prelude*, Book 2.

8. J. Eckhart, "On Detachment and Possessing God," in O. Davies, trans., *Selected Writings* (London: Penguin, 1994), 11.

9. W. S. Merwin, "Thanks," from *The Rain in the Trees*, copyright © 1988 by W. S. Merwin. Used by permission of Alfred A. Knopf, a division of Random House, Inc.

10. T. Merton, *The Springs of Contemplation* (Notre Dame, IN: Ave Maria Press, 1992), 117.

11. R. Sennett, *Flesh and Stone: The Body and the City in Western Civilisation* (London: Norton, 1994), 374.

12. Ibid., 376.

13. Quoted in J. Jacobs, *The Death and Life of Great American Cities* (New York: Random House, 1961), 2.

Chapter 6 Gift

1. G. Cray, ed., *Mission-Shaped Church: Church Planting and Fresh Expressions of Church in a Changing Context* (London: Church House Publishing, 2004), xi.

2. A. de Botton, *Status Anxiety* (London: Penguin, 2004). In this excellent book, de Botton exposes the universal desire we all have for status and how, in such "free" capitalist democracies as the US, the very freedom to be anyone and become anything has actually led to major anxiety about failure. De Botton sees orthodox Christianity as one route out of this, because it provides escape from the lies that "I am what I consume" and that success is to be judged in terms of material wealth.

3. L. Hyde, *The Gift: Imagination and the Erotic Life of Property* (London: Vintage, 1999), xiv.

4. Ibid., xi.

5. On a practical level, it is for this reason that I think that the practice of passing a collection plate during a service should be stopped immediately. As committed members of a congregation, we may be able to discern that we are making "an offering," but it is likely that this subtle distinction will be missed by any visitors, and the "gift" of the service will be destroyed.

6. Hyde, *Gift*, 18.

7. Ibid.

8. This may provide part of the answer to why creative people are found at the fringes of congregations and often don't stay long, and why many alternative worship groups have been started, and subsequently led, by creatives and—as creatives rarely make good leaders—have in the end suffered from poor leadership.

9. The wonderful exception being the deliberately corporate-free Radiohead gigs on their KidA tour in 2001.

10. H. Nouwen, *The Wounded Healer* (London: Darton, Longman & Todd, 1994), 38.

11. Hyde, *Gift*, 20.

12. Ibid.

13. Ibid., 4.

Chapter 7 Dirt

1. M. Douglas, *Purity and Danger* (London: Routledge, 1966), 50. Douglas's classic "analysis of the concept of pollution and taboo" is a major reference for these thoughts.

2. Interestingly, the Church of England has recently proposed changing the law to make parish boundaries more "permeable," to allow church planting into parishes where disgruntled incumbents are against it. See G. Cray, ed., *Mission-Shaped Church: Church Planting and Fresh Expressions of Church in a Changing Context* (London: Church House Publishing, 2004), 139.

3. J. Fowler, *Stages of Faith: The Psychology of Human Development and the Quest for Meaning* (New York: HarperCollins, 1995), 186–87.

4. C. Jung, *Memories, Dreams and Reflections*, ed. A. Jaffé (London: Fontana, 1995), 52, 56.

5. C. Jung, *Problems of Alchemy*, in A. Storr, ed., *Jung: Selected Writings* (London: Fontana Press, 1986), 258.

6. C. Barks and J. Moyne, trans., *The Essential Rumi* (London: Penguin, 1999), 116. Used with permission.

Interestingly, Rumi still appears to be playing the role of trickster: in the events following the terrorist attacks on September 11, 2001, many Americans were shocked to learn that their most-read poet was actually both a Muslim and from Afghanistan. Thus they found one whom they were in danger of labeling "dirty" in fact living among them.

7. Source unknown, quoted in L. Hyde, *Trickster Makes This World: Mischief, Myth and Art* (New York: North Point Press, 1999), 186. I

am heavily indebted for inspiration on dirt to Hyde's excellent work in this book.

8. Ibid., 187.

9. Ibid., 189. For a far more in-depth study of cultural myths like these, see Claude Lévi-Strauss's classic work, *The Raw and the Cooked: Introduction to a Science of Mythology* (London: Jonathan Cape, 1970).

10. Hyde, *Trickster*, 177.

11. Quoted in ibid., 193.

12. The following quotes from Collins are taken from Steve Collins, "How Far Is Too Far?" *Small Fire* (February 2002), found at http://ship-of-fools.com/Columns/Collins/Collins0202.html.

13. P. Larkin, "Church Going," in *The Less Deceived* (London: Marvell Press, 1955), 23.

14. Quoted in R. Andrews, ed., *The New Penguin Dictionary of Modern Quotations* (London: Penguin, 2001), 348.

Chapter 8 The Emergence of Christ

1. P. Pullman, *The Amber Spyglass* (London: Point, 2001), 548.

{ Further Reading }

In compiling the following list of books I have had to face the difficult choice of whether to categorize them or not. I have decided to do this for the sake of clarity, but, in creating order, I am aware of the impossibility of doing so without coming up against anomalies so, in the spirit of the text, please allow each reference the fluidity to cross these boundaries.

Art / Culture / Philosophy

Berger, J. *Ways of Seeing*. London: Penguin, 1990.

Booker, C. *The Neophiliacs: The Revolution in English Life in the Fifties and Sixties*. London: Pimlico, 1992.

———. *Status Anxiety*. London: Penguin, 2004.

Brook, C. *The K Foundation Burn a Million Quid*. London: Ellipsis, 1997.

Dark Star. *Beneath the Paving Stones: Situationists and the Beach, May 1968*. Edinburgh: AK Press, 2001.

Davis, E. *TechGnosis: Myth, Magic and Mysticism in the Age of Information*. London: Five Star, 2004.

de Botton, A. *The Art of Travel*. London: Penguin, 2003.

Descartes, R. *A Discourse on Method etc.* Edited by E. Rhys. London: Dent, 1912.

Douglas, M. *Purity and Danger: An Analysis of Concepts of Pollution and Taboo*. London: Routledge, 2002.

Huxley, A. *The Doors of Perception*. London: Grafton, 1977.

Hyde, L. *The Gift: Imagination and the Erotic Life of Property*. London: Vintage, 1999.

———. *Trickster Makes This World: Mischief, Myth and Art*. New York: North Point Press, 1999.

Jung, C. G. *Memories, Dreams and Reflections*. London: Fontana, 1995.

———. *Selected Writings*. Edited by A. Storr. London: Fontana, 1986.

Lévi-Strauss, C. *The Raw and the Cooked: Introduction to a Science of Mythology*. London: Jonathan Cape, 1970.

Marcuse, H. *One-Dimensional Man*. London: Routledge, 1964.

May, R. *The Courage to Create*. New York: Norton, 1994.

Ruskin, J. *Unto This Last*. London: Penguin Classics, 1985.

Tanizaki, J. *In Praise of Shadows*. London: Vintage, 2001.

Virilio, P. *Ground Zero*. London: Verso, 2002.

———. *Speed and Politics*. Translated by M. Polizzotti. New York: Semiotexte, 1986.

Whyte, J. *Bad Thoughts: A Guide to Clear Thinking*. London: Corvo, 2003.

Wolfe, T. *From Bauhaus to Our House*. London: Jonathan Cape, 1981.

———. *The Electric Kool-Aid Acid Test*. London: Black Swan, 1989.

Cities / Urban Life

Ackroyd, P. *London: The Biography*. London: Vintage, 2001.

Augé, M. *Non-places: Introduction to an Anthropology of Supermodernity*. London: Verso, 1995.

Jacobs, J. *The Death and Life of Great American Cities*. New York: Random House, 1961.

Sennett, R. *Flesh and Stone: The Body and the City in Western Civilization*. New York: W. W. Norton, 1994.

Toffler, A. *Future Shock*. London: Pan, 1971.

Complexity / Emergence

Capra, F. *The Hidden Connections: A Science for Sustainable Living*. London: Flamingo, 2003.

de Landa, M. *A Thousand Years of Nonlinear History*. New York: Zone, 1997.

Griffin, D. *The Emergence of Leadership: Linking Self-Organization and Ethics*. New York, Routledge, 2002.

Johnson, S. *Emergence: The Connected Lives of Ants, Brains, Cities and Software*. London: Penguin, 2001.

Kaplan, A. *Development Practitioners and Social Process: Artists of the Invisible*. London: Pluto Press, 2002.

McMaster, M. *The Intelligence Advantage: Organizing for Complexity*. New York: Butterworth-Heinemann, 1996.

Mitchell Waldrop, M. *Complexity*. London: Penguin, 1992.

Morrison, K. *School Leadership and Complexity Theory*. London: Routledge, 2002.

Singh, S. *Fermat's Last Theorem*. London: Fourth Estate, 1997.

Emerging Church

Baker, J., D. Gay, and J. Brown. *Alternative Worship*. London: SPCK, 2003.

Cray, G., et al. *Mission-Shaped Church: Church Planting and Fresh Expressions of Church in a Changing Context*. A report of the working group of the Church of England's Mission and Public Affairs Council. London: Church House Publishing, 2004.

Gibbs, E., and R. Bolger. *Emerging Churches: Creating Christian Community in Postmodern Cultures*. Grand Rapids: Baker, 2005.

Jamieson, A. *A Churchless Faith: Faith Journeys beyond the Churches*. London: SPCK, 2002.

Riddell, M. *Threshold of the Future: Reforming the Church in the Post-Christian West*. London: SPCK, 1998.

Rollins, P. *How (Not) to Speak of God*. Brewster: Paraclete Press, 2006.

Ward, P. *Liquid Church*. Carlisle: Paternoster, 2002.

Fiction

Dostoyevsky, F. *The Brothers Karamazov*. Translated by D. Margarshack. London: Penguin, 1958.

Endo, S. *Silence*. Translated by W. Johnston. Marlboro, NJ: Taplinger, 1980.

McGregor, J. *If Nobody Speaks of Remarkable Things*. London: Bloomsbury, 2003.

Pullman, P. *His Dark Materials Trilogy: Northern Lights, The Subtle Knife, The Amber Spyglass*. London: Scholastic, 1998–2000.

Poetry

Hafiz. *The Gift: Poems by Hafiz, The Great Sufi Master*. Translated by D. Ladinsky. London: Compass, 1999.

Larkin, P. *Collected Poems*. London: Faber & Faber, 2003.

Merwin, W. S. *The Rain in the Trees*. New York: Alfred Knopf, 1999.

Rilke, R. M. *Rilke's Book of Hours: Love Poems to God*. Translated by A. Barrows and J. Macy. New York: Riverhead, 1996.

Rumi. *The Essential Rumi*. Translated by C. Barks. London: Penguin, 1999.

Thomas, R. S. *Collected Poems 1945–1990*. London: Dent, 1993.

Wordsworth, W. *The Prelude*. Edited by E. de Selincourt. Oxford: Oxford University Press, 1970.

Spirituality

Clément, O., ed. *The Roots of Christian Mysticism*. New York: New City Press, 1996.

Eckhart, J. *Selected Writings*. Edited by O. Davies. London: Penguin, 1994.

Fowler, J. *Faithful Change: The Personal and Public Challenges of Postmodern Life*. Nashville: Abingdon Press, 1996.

———. *Stages of Faith: The Psychology of Human Development and the Quest for Meaning*. New York: HarperCollins, 1981.

Fox, M. *Creation Spirituality: Liberating Gifts for the People of the Earth*. New York: HarperCollins, 1991.

McIntosh, M. *Mysteries of Faith*. Boston: Cowley, 2000.

Merton, T. *The Intimate Merton: His Life from His Journals*. Edited by P. Hart and J. Montaldo. New York: Lion, 1999.

———. *New Seeds of Contemplation*. New York: New Directions, 1972.

———. *The Seven Storey Mountain*. London: SPCK, 1990.

———. *The Springs of Contemplation: A Retreat at the Abbey of Gethsemani*. Notre Dame, IN: Ave Maria Press, 1992.

Nouwen, H. *The Return of the Prodigal Son*. London: Darton, Longman & Todd, 1994.

———. *The Wounded Healer*. London: Darton, Longman & Todd, 1994.

Rohr, R. *Simplicity: The Art of Living*. New York: Crossroad Publishing, 1991.

Williams, R. *Writing in the Dust: Reflections on 11th September and Its Aftermath*. London: Hodder & Stoughton, 2002.

Theology

Brueggemann, W. *Hopeful Imagination: Prophetic Voices in Exile*. London: SCM, 1986.

———. *The Prophetic Imagination*. Minneapolis: Fortress, 1978.

———. *Texts Under Negotiation: The Bible and the Postmodern Imagination*. Minneapolis: Augsburg Fortress, 1993.

Chesterton, G. K. *Orthodoxy*. London: House of Stratus, 2001.

Fee, G. *Paul, the Spirit and the People of God*. Massachusetts: Hendrickson, 1996.

Miles, J. *God: A Biography*. London: Touchstone, 1998.

Wink, W. *The Powers That Be: Theology for a New Millennium*. Minneapolis: Augsburg Fortress, 1998.

Kester Brewin teaches mathematics and religious studies in a London high school, just across the road from his house. He also writes on education, including a report for the influential think-tank *Demos* on government policy and school transformation. Born into a vicarage in 1972, he has been deeply involved in the church ever since, and his passion to see it reincarnated has led him down myriad ecclesiastic avenues. In 1998 he co-created the "Dreamspace" weekend in London, out of which the alternative worship group Vaux was born. A collective of artists and city-lovers, Vaux has been exploring urban theology through various media ever since. Kester is married with two young children; he used to find time to enjoy reading and short film production, and has somehow recently found the time to finish his first novel.

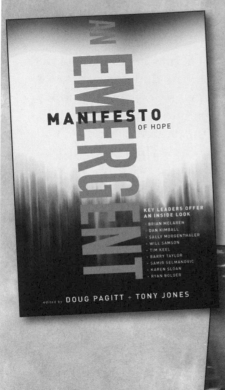

>>>>>>>>>>>>>>>>>>>>>>>>>>>>

for the latest ēmersion releases.

**Justice in the Burbs:
Being the Hands of Jesus
Wherever You Live**
by Will and Lisa Samson

**Intuitive Leadership:
Embracing a Paradigm of
Narrative, Metaphor, & Chaos**
by Tim Keel

ēmersion
a partnership between:

www.bakerbooks.com

emergent village